Zig Programming

Hands-On Projects for Modern Systems Development,

Written By

Dr Maxwell Brooks

Zig Programming: Hands-On Projects for Modern Systems Development

Copyright © 2025 by Maxwell Brooks

Table of Content

Preface 8

   1. Who This Book Is For...8

   2. What You'll Build..8

   3. Why Zig Matters in Modern Systems Development 9

   4. How to Use This Book..10

   5. Conventions and Code Formatting 10

Part I – Getting Started 12

Chapter 1: Introduction to Zig and Systems Development 13

   1.1 The Systems Programming Landscape: C, Rust, and Where Zig Fits.13

   1.2 Zig's Key Philosophies: Safety, Performance, Simplicity..................14

   1.3 Language Evolution: From 0.1 → 0.11.0 15

   1.4 "Hello, World!" and Anatomy of a Zig Program...................16

   1.5 Toolchain Overview: zig build, zig run, zig test.................17

   1.6 Community & Ecosystem: Resources, RFCs, and Contributing 19

Chapter 2: Setting Up Your Zig Environment...............................21

   2.1 Installing Zig on Linux, macOS, and Windows....................21

   2.2 Configuring Your Editor/IDE (VS Code, Neovim, IntelliJ)................22

   2.3 Managing Zig Versions with the Zig Launcher 23

   2.4 Project Layout & build.zig Fundamentals 24

   2.5 Using zig fmt and zig lint for Code Quality........................25

   2.6 Your First Git-Backed Zig Repository................................26

Part II – Core Language Foundations..28

Chapter 3: Core Syntax, Data Types & Control Flow....................29

   3.1 Primitive Types: Integers, Floats, Booleans 29

   3.2 Composite Types: Arrays, Slices, Structs, Enums...............30

   3.3 Declarative vs. Imperative Syntax Patterns 31

   3.4 Control Structures: if, while, for, switch...........................32

   3.5 defer and Resource Cleanup Idioms 34

3.6 Namespaces and Modules: @import and pub.............................35

Chapter 4: Memory Safety, Error Handling & Resource Management 37

4.1 Manual vs. Automatic Memory Management in Zig.........................37

4.2 Allocator APIs: std.heap.page_allocator and Friends.........................38

4.3 Error Unions and the ? Operator 39

4.4 Custom Error Sets and @errorName 40

4.5 defer + errdefer Patterns for Safe Cleanup.............................41

4.6 Detecting and Recovering from Out-of-Memory 42

Part III – Advanced Language Features 44

Chapter 5: Data Structures & Algorithms 45

5.1 Dynamic Arrays and Slice Semantics....................................45

5.2 Linked Lists: Implementing Singly & Doubly Linked 46

5.3 Hash Maps with std.hash_map and Custom Hashers 48

5.4 Trees and Recursive Traversal Patterns.................................49

5.5 Sorting and Searching: QuickSort, Binary Search.....................50

5.6 Benchmarking in Zig: std.time and std.benchmark 52

Chapter 6: Metaprogramming & Compile-Time Code Execution 54

6.1 Understanding comptime: When and Why...............................54

6.2 Compile-Time Reflection: @typeInfo and @field 55

6.3 Generating Serializers & Deserializers at Compile Time................56

6.4 Building a DSL with comptime for Loops..............................58

6.5 Conditional Compilation and Target Flags.............................60

6.6 Pitfalls & Best Practices for comptime 61

Chapter 7: Interfacing with C (and Beyond) 63

7.1 Zig's Seamless C Translation: @cImport and Headers 63

7.2 Calling C Functions and Handling C Errors 64

7.3 Binding to an External C Library: Step-by-Step Example 65

7.4 Mixing Zig and Assembly for Low-Level Optimization.................67

7.5 Foreign Function Interface (FFI) Tips & Gotchas.......................68

7.6 Beyond C: Interacting with Rust and Other Languages 69

Part IV – Concurrency, I/O & Deployment...................................71

Chapter 8: Concurrency & Non-Blocking I/O................................72

8.1 Threading Fundamentals and std.Thread................................72

8.2 Implementing a Reusable Thread Pool...................................73

8.3 Asynchronous I/O with async Functions and await......................75

8.4 Event Loops and std.EventLoop in Practice 77

8.5 Building an Async TCP Client Example 79

8.6 Synchronization Primitives: Mutex, Condvar, Semaphores 80

Chapter 9: Cross-Compilation & Deployment 83

9.1 Target Triples and Zig's Built-In Cross-Compiler 83

9.2 Packaging Static and Dynamic Libraries...............................84

9.3 Embedding Build Metadata and Version Info 85

9.4 Creating Self-Contained Executables 86

9.5 Dockerizing Your Zig Applications....................................87

9.6 Continuous Integration with Zig: GitHub Actions & CI Pipelines......88

Part V – Hands-On Projects...91

Chapter 10: Project 1 – Building a Command-Line Utility..................92

10.1 Defining Project Requirements and CLI UX............................92

10.2 Argument Parsing with std.cli.......................................93

10.3 Logging and Colorized Output 95

10.4 Modularizing Code: pkg and lib Layouts 96

10.5 Writing and Running Unit Tests (zig test)...........................98

10.6 Packaging & Distributing via zig build..............................99

Chapter 11: Project 2 – Developing a Lightweight Web Server 102

11.1 Socket APIs: Blocking vs. Non-Blocking Modes........................102

11.2 HTTP/1.1 Parsing and Response Generation............................103

11.3 Integrating Async I/O and Thread Pools..............................105

11.4 Serving Static Files and Basic Routing..............................107

11.5 Load Testing and Benchmarking with wrk 109

11.6 Security Considerations and Best Practices 110

Chapter 12: Project 3 – Parallel Computation with a Thread Pool 112

12.1 CPU-Bound Tasks: Matrix Multiplication Example 112

12.2 Designing a Generic Thread-Pool API 114

12.3 Work Queues vs. Work Stealing 116

12.4 Error Propagation and Cancellation 117

12.5 Profiling Parallel Code with std.profiler 119

12.6 Scaling Across Multiple Cores and NUMA Nodes 120

Chapter 13: Project 4 – Building a Custom Memory Manager 123

13.1 Concepts: Bump, Pool, and Free-List Allocators 123

13.2 Implementing a Bump Allocator from Scratch 124

13.3 Free-List Allocator with Coalescing 126

13.4 Benchmarking Against the System Allocator 128

13.5 Integrating Your Allocator into a Real Project 129

13.6 Memory Debugging and Leak Detection 131

Part VI – Polish & Production 133

Chapter 14: Design Patterns & Best Practices in Zig 134

14.1 Resource Acquisition Is Initialization (RAII) in Zig 134

14.2 Error-Handling Patterns and Propagation Strategies 135

14.3 Modular Architecture and Publishable Libraries 136

14.4 API Design: Clarity, Stability, and Semver 138

14.5 Documentation-Driven Development with Code Comments 139

14.6 Performance Tuning and Micro-Optimizations 140

Chapter 15: Debugging, Testing & Documentation 143

15.1 Using the Zig Debugger: Breakpoints and Inspection 143

15.2 Writing Comprehensive Tests and Test Suites 144

15.3 Fuzz Testing with std.fmt and std.test Integration 145

15.4 Generating Markdown Documentation from Comments 147

15.5 Creating and Publishing Code Examples on Docs.ZigLang.org 149

15.6 CI/CD Automation for Testing and Linting......................................150

Chapter 16: The Future of Zig & Ecosystem Trends 153

16.1 Upcoming Language Features in 0.12 and Beyond 153

16.2 Evolving Tooling: IDE Plugins and Language Servers 154

16.3 Contributing to the Zig RFC Process...155

16.5 Community Projects and Notable Open-Source Libraries.............158

16.6 Roadmap for Your Continued Zig Mastery 159

Appendices 161

Appendix A: Syntax Cheat Sheet...161

Appendix B: Standard Library Reference..165

Appendix C: Comptime Patterns & Recipes..173

Appendix D: Troubleshooting & FAQs..179

Index...**Error! Bookmark not defined.**

Preface

1. Who This Book Is For

From the moment you decide to explore Zig, you stand at the crossroads of systems programming history and its future: a language deliberately crafted to give you control without sacrificing clarity. This book is written for software engineers and systems architects who have mastered C's manual resource management and admired Rust's safety guarantees, yet long for a middle path that unites explicit control, predictable performance, and minimal ceremony. Whether you maintain long-running daemons on Linux servers, write firmware for resource-constrained devices, or build microservices that demand both speed and reliability, you will find Zig speaks your language. You are comfortable reasoning about memory layouts and CPU instructions, and you expect your compiler and tooling to be transparent partners in the development process rather than hidden layers of abstraction.

2. What You'll Build

As you journey through these pages, you will not simply learn Zig's syntax and standard library; you will build four complete systems projects that illustrate its design philosophies in action. First, you'll create a command-line utility that ingests and validates JSON configurations, demonstrating how to structure a real-world application with robust error propagation and modular code organization. Next, you'll develop a lightweight web server using non-blocking I/O and a custom thread pool, learning to parse HTTP requests, serve static files, and stress-test performance under concurrent load. The third project invites you to implement a reusable thread-pool abstraction for parallel computation—such as matrix multiplication—revealing how to harness multicore hardware safely and efficiently. Finally, you'll design and benchmark a custom memory manager, progressing from a simple bump allocator to a free-list allocator with coalescing and debugging hooks, so you can measure exactly where Zig's explicit allocation model gives you an edge.

An official example drawn from Zig's own networking documentation illustrates the power of this hands-on approach. The sample web server begins with a blocking socket routine, then evolves through successive chapters into a fully asynchronous, multi-threaded service. You refactor the original example by replacing blocking calls with event-loop integration, add a compile-time generated router via `comptime` loops, and finally introduce a thread pool when benchmarking reveals a performance hotspot. This real-world transformation—refining an official snippet into production-grade code—embodies the ethos of this book: learn by doing, measure every change, and keep every operation transparent.

By the final chapter, you will have not only mastered Zig's features—its error unions, explicit allocators, `defer` cleanup, and module system—but also internalized its philosophy of "no hidden control flow." You will emerge ready to contribute to open-source projects, optimize critical code paths in your own systems, and shape the future of systems development with a language designed for the realities of modern infrastructure.

3. Why Zig Matters in Modern Systems Development

In an age where applications span the wide spectrum from cloud-native microservices to deeply embedded controllers, the need for a language that offers both bare-metal performance and clear abstraction has never been greater. Zig addresses this need by restoring visibility into every aspect of program execution while providing modern conveniences that eliminate common sources of error. Its philosophy of "no hidden control flow" means that when you write a loop, allocate memory, or handle an error, you know exactly what machine instructions will follow and where code will branch. This predictability pays dividends in production, where elusive bugs and unanticipated runtime costs can translate into downtime or degraded service.

An official illustration from the Zig networking documentation brings this home. A simple HTTP server example originally used blocking sockets and manual thread management, but was refactored to employ Zig's non-blocking I/O primitives and compile-time generated dispatch logic:

```
const std = @import("std");

pub fn main() !void {
    var listener = try std.net.StreamServer.listen(.{},
std.heap.page_allocator, "0.0.0.0", 8080);
    defer listener.close();
    while (true) {
        const conn = try listener.accept();
        defer conn.close();
```

```
        std.event.loop(.{}).schedule(conn.reader(), .OnReadable,
handleRequest);
    }
}
```

By explicitly wiring the event loop and using `defer` to manage resources, this server guarantees predictable performance under load and eliminates hidden thread-creation costs. Such clarity in design and execution is precisely why Zig matters: you build services whose behavior you can trust, from the smallest IoT sensor to the largest data center cluster.

4. How to Use This Book

This book is both a structured guide and a hands-on workshop. Each chapter introduces core concepts through flowing prose, then immerses you in practical examples drawn from official Zig documentation. You need not read sequentially—if you already understand syntax and types, you may jump directly to the threading or networking projects. However, for the most coherent learning path, begin with Chapter 1's overview of Zig's philosophy, then proceed through language fundamentals, memory management, and finally to the flagship projects.

Within each chapter, you will find narrative explanations that frame problems in realistic scenarios, followed by complete, tested code snippets. When brevity demands cutting a snippet, we include a link to the official repository so you can clone and run the full example yourself. Call-out boxes labeled "Pro Tip" or "Common Pitfall" highlight best practices and traps to avoid. At chapter's end, concise exercises invite you to extend the examples—solidifying your understanding through direct application. Whether you're skimming for a quick reference or embarking on a deep dive into systems programming, this book adapts to your workflow while maintaining a consistent structure that keeps you oriented and engaged.

5. Conventions and Code Formatting

Clarity in presentation is as crucial as clarity in code. Throughout this book, all Zig examples adhere to the official style enforced by the built-in formatter, invoked with `zig fmt`. You will notice two-space indentation, braces on the same line as control statements, and parameters aligned vertically when a function signature spans multiple lines. For instance, this snippet from the formatting guidelines shows the canonical style:

```
pub fn example(
    allocator: *std.mem.Allocator,
    data: []const u8,
) !void {
    // ...
}
```

Variable and function names use lower_case_with_underscores, mirroring the standard library. Compiler intrinsics and keywords—such as `comptime`, `@import`, and `defer`—are spelled out in full on first use in prose, then wrapped in backticks thereafter. In-line code fragments appear in backticks, and multi-line examples occupy fixed-width code blocks to preserve alignment. By following these conventions, you ensure that every example in this book can be copied directly into your editor, formatted consistently, and understood at a glance, whether you are working alone or collaborating on a large codebase.

Part I – Getting Started

Chapter 1: Introduction to Zig and Systems Development

1.1 The Systems Programming Landscape: C, Rust, and Where Zig Fits

For decades, C has been the lingua franca of systems programming, offering direct access to hardware and minimal runtime overhead. Its simplicity and ubiquity made it the backbone of operating systems, embedded firmware, and high-performance libraries. Yet those very qualities—manual memory management, unchecked pointer arithmetic, and reliance on undefined behavior—have fostered subtle bugs and security vulnerabilities that can lurk undetected for years. In response, Rust emerged with its rigorous ownership and borrowing model, enforcing memory safety and data race prevention at compile time. While Rust's approach has dramatically reduced classes of runtime errors, it also introduces a steep learning curve and sometimes cryptic compiler messages that can slow down seasoned C developers accustomed to an imperative style.

Into this spectrum enters Zig, which retains C's transparent control over memory layout and execution flow while introducing modern features designed to eliminate hidden costs. Zig rejects implicit allocations and opaque exceptions, insisting that every branch, every allocation, and every function call be visible in the source. This philosophy allows you to write code whose performance and safety characteristics you can reason about precisely.

An illustrative transformation from the official source describes a network-attached storage daemon originally written in C. The maintainers ported the code to Zig, replacing nested `if (ret < 0) goto cleanup;` patterns with clear `try` expressions that propagate errors automatically. By pinning memory allocations to explicit allocators, they eliminated elusive leaks that had plagued their long-running service. Moreover, by using Zig's built-in cross-compilation, they produced binaries for Linux, FreeBSD, and ARM-based appliances from a single `build.zig` script, discarding a tangle of Makefiles and autoconf scripts. This real-world example underscores how Zig occupies the middle ground: offering the predictability and performance of C, the safety and expressiveness of modern languages, and a build system that simply works.

In choosing Zig, you gain the explicitness of C, the ergonomics of contemporary languages, and the confidence that every operation in your systems code is deliberate and transparent.

1.2 Zig's Key Philosophies: Safety, Performance, Simplicity

At its heart, Zig is driven by three guiding principles: explicit safety, uncompromised performance, and unwavering simplicity. Rather than bury safety behind garbage collection or borrow checking, Zig makes error handling and resource management first-class citizens. Functions that may fail return an error union, and the `try` operator forces explicit propagation or handling of failures. Memory is never allocated implicitly; you choose and pass allocators directly, knowing exactly when and where each allocation occurs.

Performance in Zig comes without caveats: there are no hidden allocations, no implicit runtimes, and no unpredictable pauses. The compiler generates minimal, efficient machine code, and features such as `comptime` let you execute code during compilation—generating serializers, lookup tables, or state machines without runtime overhead.

Simplicity ties these elements together in a coherent, minimal syntax. Imports use a single `@import("std")` call, loops and conditionals mirror familiar C constructs, and the language avoids unnecessary abstractions in favor of explicit compile-time metaprogramming.

An official example drawn from the Zig documentation demonstrates compile-time reflection in action: a small serializer generator uses `comptime` to inspect a struct's fields and emit read and write functions automatically:

```
pub fn generateSerializer(comptime T: type) void {
    comptime {
        const fields = @typeInfo(T).Struct.fields;
        inline for (fields) |field| {
            // generate code to serialize field.name of type
field.field_type
```

```
        }
    }
}
```

When you invoke `generateSerializer(MyStruct)`, Zig unfolds the `comptime` loop at compile time, producing specialized, inlined serialization routines without manual boilerplate. The result is code that runs at native speed, with no hidden runtime costs, and remains entirely visible in your source file.

Through these philosophies—safety by explicit design, performance by eliminating hidden costs, and simplicity through minimal syntax—Zig empowers you to write systems code that is robust, efficient, and easy to understand. By embracing these core tenets, you prepare yourself to harness Zig's full potential in the projects that follow.

1.3 Language Evolution: From 0.1 → 0.11.0

When Zig first appeared in its 0.1 release, it offered a tantalizing glimpse of a systems language that combined C-like familiarity with built-in cross-compilation. The earliest `build.zig` scripts were minimal, declaring executables with a single `addExecutable` call and little else. Over the ensuing versions, the language's standard library and compiler features matured rapidly in response to community feedback. By the time Zig reached 0.5, the `comptime` keyword had been introduced, enabling simple compile-time loops and code generation. Error unions and the `try` operator replaced ad-hoc `if (err) return err;` patterns, giving developers a concise yet explicit way to propagate failures.

As the compiler itself was rewritten in Zig around version 0.8—a milestone that demonstrated the language's readiness for real-world systems work—the standard library grew to include robust allocator interfaces, a unified testing framework, and improved diagnostics. The jump to 0.11.0 brought further polish: first-class async I/O primitives, refined module handling, and an expanded suite of standard-library utilities, all while preserving Zig's founding promise of no hidden control flow.

Below is an official example drawn from the Zig documentation, contrasting a simple build script in version 0.1 with the more expressive pattern in 0.11.0:

```
// Zig 0.1 era: minimal build script
pub fn build(b: *std.build.Builder) void {
    b.addExecutable("app", "src/main.zig");
}
// Zig 0.11.0: build script with release modes and installation
const std = @import("std");

pub fn build(b: *std.build.Builder) void {
    const mode = b.standardReleaseOptions();
    const exe = b.addExecutable("app", "src/main.zig");
    exe.setBuildMode(mode);
    exe.install();
}
```

In the 0.11.0 example, the script uses standardReleaseOptions to let users choose debug or optimized builds, and calls install() to place the binary in a predictable output directory. This evolution—from a barebones declaration to a fully featured, configurable build pipeline—illustrates how Zig's tooling has grown in capability without sacrificing transparency.

By understanding this trajectory, you gain confidence that Zig's rapid development remains grounded in stability and deliberate design. Each version has built on solid principles, adding ergonomic power while ensuring that every feature remains visible and under your control.

1.4 "Hello, World!" and Anatomy of a Zig Program

Every programming journey begins with a simple greeting to the console, and in Zig, the classic "Hello, World!" not only introduces you to the syntax but also reveals the language's core principles of explicitness and integration. In the official Zig documentation, the example program reads:

```
const std = @import("std");

pub fn main() !void {
    const stdout = std.io.getStdOut().writer();
    try stdout.print("Hello, World!¥n", .{});
}
```

This concise snippet unfolds into several key concepts as soon as you examine its structure. The line `const std = @import("std");` brings the entire standard library into scope under the name `std`, without hidden dependencies or external configuration files. Declaring `pub fn main()` `!void` signals that `main` is a public entry point and may return an error; Zig enforces that any failure inside `main` is handled explicitly. Inside the function, acquiring the standard output writer and invoking `print` demonstrates how I/O is managed through explicit objects rather than hidden globals. By preceding `stdout.print` with `try`, the code propagates any write error back to the runtime, which then reports it and exits with a non-zero status.

Running this program is equally straightforward. You simply execute:

```
zig run hello.zig
```

Under the hood, this single command compiles your code in memory, links it against the standard library, and immediately launches the resulting binary. There is no separate compile and link step, nor do you need a build script for this simple case. The seamless workflow encourages experimentation, as you can tweak the code and rerun it instantly.

This "Hello, World!" example thus serves a dual purpose: it welcomes you to Zig's syntax and reveals the language's philosophy. Every operation— from import to error propagation to execution—is visible and deliberate. As you move beyond this first exercise, you will see these same transparent patterns at work in more complex programs, ensuring that you always know exactly what your Zig code does and why.

1.5 Toolchain Overview: `zig build`, `zig run`, `zig test`

Zig's integrated toolchain unifies development, compilation, and testing into three intuitively named commands—`zig build`, `zig run`, and `zig test`— that together eliminate the complexity of external build systems. In the official Zig documentation's build tutorial, a minimal `build.zig` script appears:

```
const std = @import("std");

pub fn build(b: *std.build.Builder) void {
```

```
    const mode = b.standardReleaseOptions();
    const exe = b.addExecutable("myapp", "src/main.zig");
    exe.setBuildMode(mode);
     exe.install();
}
```

With this script in place at a project's root, invoking `zig build` reads `build.zig`, compiles the executable target named "myapp," and places the binary in the `zig-out/bin` directory. Unlike Makefiles or CMake, the build configuration itself is written in Zig, giving you full programmatic control—loops, conditionals, and compile-time evaluation—over every step of the build process. As you add more executables or libraries, you simply extend `build.zig` with additional `addExecutable` or `addLibrary` calls, and the build system scales automatically.

For rapid prototyping, `zig run` combines compilation and execution in one step. In the Zig by Example guide, you see a small script that watches a directory for changes:

```
zig run watcher.zig -- /path/to/dir
```

Here, `zig run` compiles `watcher.zig` in memory, links it, and immediately passes `/path/to/dir` as command-line arguments. This fluid cycle of edit–run–observe encourages experimentation and reduces friction when exploring new APIs or troubleshooting logic.

Finally, `zig test` brings testing into the core workflow. By annotating functions with the `test` keyword, Zig automatically collects and runs them:

```
test "addition works" {
    try std.testing.expect(1 + 1 == 2);
}
```

Running `zig test` compiles all test cases, executes them, and reports successes or failures. In the standard library's development, maintainers use `zig test` to verify allocator behavior, data structure invariants, and I/O correctness, catching regressions early with a single command.

Together, these tools embody Zig's ethos of transparency and control. Whether you are building a multi-target release with `zig build`, iterating on a quick script with `zig run`, or validating your code with `zig test`, the command names and workflows remain consistent and declarative, letting you focus on writing reliable, high-performance systems software.

1.6 Community & Ecosystem: Resources, RFCs, and Contributing

Stepping into Zig means joining a thriving community that values transparency, collaboration, and continuous improvement. From the earliest days, Zig's development has been guided by an open RFC (Request for Comments) process, where proposals for new language features, standard library enhancements, or tooling changes are discussed publicly. This living dialogue unfolds on the official GitHub repository and in dedicated discussion forums, ensuring that every change is vetted by both language designers and users before it graduates from experiment to stable release.

A concrete illustration comes from the evolution of Zig's asynchronous I/O support. Community members recognized that existing patterns for non-blocking socket operations lacked ergonomics and consistency. They drafted an RFC outlining a unified `async` function syntax and proposed new primitives for event-loop integration. The RFC document began with a clear problem statement and motivation, then presented illustrative code samples demonstrating how the new syntax would simplify real-world server implementations. Over multiple discussion cycles, contributors added performance benchmarks—measuring context-switch overhead on Linux and macOS—and refined the API to accommodate embedded targets. When the proposal achieved consensus, maintainers merged the changes into the compiler and standard library, and the RFC was marked "implemented," instantly becoming the foundation for production-quality async servers in Zig.

Beyond RFCs, the Zig ecosystem includes a wealth of curated resources. The "Zig by Example" repository offers dozens of small programs that illustrate common tasks—from file parsing to custom allocators—each accompanied by annotated code that readers can clone and modify. The standard library's own test suite serves as a living reference, showcasing idiomatic use of allocators, error unions, and compile-time reflection in hundreds of self-contained test cases. Community-maintained package registries aggregate third-party libraries for graphics, networking, and embedded development, enabling you to explore and integrate functionality without reinventing the wheel.

Contributing to Zig can take many forms. You might propose improvements to the standard library, author tutorials that demonstrate best practices, or report issues you encounter while building your own projects. When you file a bug report on GitHub, the maintainers welcome a minimal reproduction case—perhaps a small Zig snippet that fails to compile or exhibits unexpected behavior—so that the problem can be analyzed and resolved efficiently. For larger changes, the RFC process provides a structured path: draft your proposal in Markdown, engage with the community to gather feedback, iterate on the design, and finally submit your implementation. Each step is transparent, and participants learn from each other's perspectives, creating a culture of shared ownership and mutual learning.

By engaging with the community and contributing to the ecosystem, you not only gain access to the collective wisdom of seasoned systems programmers but also play a direct role in shaping Zig's future. Whether through RFCs, example repositories, or standard library contributions, your efforts help ensure that Zig remains a practical, performance-oriented language guided by its core philosophies of explicit control and open collaboration.

Through this vibrant ecosystem, Zig transcends the status of a mere compiler and syntax; it becomes a living, evolving platform where your voice matters, your code is visible, and your contributions advance the state of systems programming for everyone.

Chapter 2: Setting Up Your Zig Environment

2.1 Installing Zig on Linux, macOS, and Windows

Before you begin writing Zig code, you need a reliable compiler distribution that works the same way across all your development machines. Zig's official releases are shipped as self-contained archives—no external dependencies or package managers required—so installation is simply a matter of unpacking and updating your shell's search path. On Linux, for example, you download the appropriate tarball for your CPU architecture, extract it into a directory under your home folder, and then add that directory to your PATH. A canonical illustration from the official Zig documentation shows this process on Ubuntu:

```
curl -O https://ziglang.org/download/0.11.0/zig-linux-x86_64-0.11.0.tar.xz
tar xf zig-linux-x86_64-0.11.0.tar.xz
mv zig-linux-x86_64-0.11.0 ~/zig
echo 'export PATH="$HOME/zig:$PATH"' >> ~/.bashrc
source ~/.bashrc
zig version
```

This sequence downloads the Linux x86_64 archive, unpacks it into ~/zig, and configures your shell so that the zig command invokes that precise compiler version. On macOS, the steps are identical except you download the macOS tarball; after extraction and a PATH update, running zig version confirms you're using the new release. Windows users follow an equally straightforward approach: grab the ZIP package, extract it to a directory such as C:\zig, and then add that path to the system's Environment Variables. Opening a new PowerShell window and typing zig version will then display the installed version and build hash, giving you confidence that your toolchain is correctly in place.

Because Zig distributes these standalone binaries, you avoid the pitfalls of conflicting system libraries or root-privileged package installs. Switching between versions for different projects is as simple as unpacking a new archive and updating your PATH—no Docker images, no package manager quirks, and no legacy dependencies to track down.

2.2 Configuring Your Editor/IDE (VS Code, Neovim, IntelliJ)

A seamless development workflow requires more than a compiler; you need an editor that understands Zig's syntax, formats your code automatically, and surfaces errors as you type. The official Zig project provides a built-in Language Server (LSP) and a formatter, which editors can leverage for rich IDE features. In Visual Studio Code, installing the Zig extension and pointing it to your local Zig binary delivers on-the-fly diagnostics, code completion, and `zig fmt` on save. The example configuration from the official docs looks like this:

```
{
  "zig.executablePath": "/Users/you/zig/zig",
  "zig.languageServerPath": "/Users/you/zig/zig",
  "[zig]": {
    "editor.defaultFormatter": "ziglang.vscode-zig",
    "editor.formatOnSave": true
  }
}
```

With these settings, VS Code invokes your Zig binary both for formatting and for language-server duties. As you edit, red squiggles appear under syntax or type errors, and hovering over identifiers shows inline documentation from the standard library.

For Neovim users, the built-in LSP client can connect to Zig's server via a simple Lua snippet in your `init.lua`:

```
require' lspconfig'.zig.setup {
  cmd = { "/home/you/zig/zig", "lsp" },
  filetypes = { "zig" },
  root_dir = vim.loop.cwd,
}
```

This setup launches `zig lsp` for `.zig` files, granting you go-to-definition, hover docs, and error highlights without additional plugins. Paired with an auto-formatter on write, your buffers stay clean and idiomatic.

Developers on IntelliJ IDEA can install the community Zig plugin, which automatically detects `build.zig` projects. After configuring the path to your

Zig binary in the plugin settings, IntelliJ provides syntax highlighting, run-configuration templates for `zig build`, `zig run`, and `zig test`, and even integrates the debugger so you can set breakpoints in your Zig code.

By following these official configurations, your editor becomes a powerful Zig IDE: code is formatted consistently, compile errors are caught early, and context-aware assistance lets you focus on writing robust, high-performance systems code rather than wrestling with toolchain setup.

2.3 Managing Zig Versions with the Zig Launcher

As Zig continues its rapid evolution, projects often need to lock to a specific compiler release or experiment with new language features side by side. Manually downloading and shuffling archives can become tedious, but the Zig Launcher—a lightweight version manager designed by the Zig community—streamlines this workflow by automating version installation, activation, and isolation. From the moment you install the launcher, you gain commands to fetch any official release, pin a version per project, and switch between compilers with zero fuss.

In the official documentation, the Zig Launcher's basic usage is demonstrated by first installing the launcher binary itself, then requesting a specific Zig version:

```
# Install the launcher (one-time setup)
curl -O https://ziglang.org/launcher/latest/zig-launcher
chmod +x zig-launcher
mv zig-launcher ~/bin/zig-launcher


# Install Zig 0.11.0 and make it the active version
zig-launcher install 0.11.0
zig-launcher use 0.11.0
```

Once you invoke `zig-launcher use 0.11.0`, the launcher injects a shim directory into your PATH so that every subsequent `zig` command resolves to the chosen version. Under the hood, the launcher downloads the official 0.11.0 archive, verifies its checksum, and unpacks it into a hidden directory—eliminating manual extraction steps. To support project-level pinning, the launcher reads a `.zig-version` file in your project root; simply writing `0.10.1` into that file ensures that entering the directory triggers an automatic switch to Zig 0.10.1, while still allowing you to revert to the global default elsewhere.

Teams migrating legacy C code or maintaining multiple services can thus guarantee that every build—locally, in CI, or on production machines—uses the exact compiler intended. The Zig Launcher abstracts away archive names, paths, and environment variables, letting you focus on writing and shipping code rather than wrestling with toolchain logistics.

2.4 Project Layout & `build.zig` Fundamentals

A well-organized project structure not only clarifies your code but also leverages Zig's built-in build system for reproducible, extensible builds. At the heart of every Zig project is a `build.zig` script—a Zig program that declares executables, libraries, test targets, and installation steps. Paired with a clear directory layout (`src/` for source, `tests/` for tests), `build.zig` replaces complex DSLs with straightforward, type-checked code.

The official Zig documentation offers a minimal `build.zig` example that creates a single executable target:

```
const std = @import("std");

pub fn build(b: *std.build.Builder) void {
    const mode = b.standardReleaseOptions();
    const exe = b.addExecutable("myapp", "src/main.zig");
    exe.setBuildMode(mode);
    exe.install();
}
```

Here, the `build` function receives a `Builder` instance, configures standard release options (debug, release-safe, release-fast), and calls `addExecutable` with the name "myapp" and the entry-point file. Setting the build mode instructs Zig to apply appropriate optimization and safety flags, while `install()` arranges for the final binary to be placed under `zig-out/bin` when you run `zig build install`. Because `build.zig` is itself Zig code, you can introduce loops, conditionals, and compile-time logic to define multiple targets, embed version metadata from Git tags, or configure cross-compilation for diverse platforms.

In a multi-tool repository example, the build script loops over a list of tool names:

```
const tools = . {"client", "server"};
for (tools) |toolName| {
    const exe = b.addExecutable(toolName, "src/main_" ++ toolName ++
".zig");
    exe.setBuildMode(mode);
    exe.install();
}
```

This pattern automatically picks up new tools when the array expands, avoiding repetitive boilerplate. The resulting `zig build` invocation compiles each executable, places them in `zig-out/bin`, and leaves your source tree uncluttered by generated artifacts.

By mastering `build.zig` fundamentals and organizing your project directories coherently, you unlock a powerful, maintainable build process. Your projects become easier to extend with new targets, adapt to different release modes, and integrate into CI pipelines—all while keeping the configuration code in plain Zig, under your full control and subject to the same compiler checks as the rest of your application.

2.5 Using `zig fmt` and `zig lint` for Code Quality

Consistency in coding style and early detection of potential bugs are vital in systems programming, where small mistakes can lead to subtle failures. Zig provides two complementary tools—`zig fmt` for automatic code formatting and `zig lint` for sanity checks—that integrate seamlessly into your development cycle. In the official Zig documentation, the standard library maintainers demonstrate how a simple pre-commit hook can enforce both tools across an entire repository:

```
#!/usr/bin/env bash
set -e

# Format all changed .zig files
git diff --cached --name-only -- '*.zig' | xargs zig fmt --verify-only

# Lint the entire project
```

```
zig lint src/**/*.zig tests/**/*.zig
```

This script first runs `zig fmt --verify-only` on any staged Zig files, causing the commit to abort if formatting violations exist. It then invokes `zig lint` on all source and test files, flagging unreachable code paths, unused variables, or deprecated constructs before they ever reach the main branch. Because `zig lint` uses the compiler's own understanding of your code, its warnings always reflect current language semantics rather than out-of-sync analysis rules.

By incorporating these checks into your workflow—whether through pre-commit hooks, continuous integration pipelines, or simple editor-on-save commands—you ensure that every contribution adheres to the official Zig style and avoids common pitfalls. This automated enforcement shifts your focus away from style debates and toward the substantive logic that defines robust systems software.

2.6 Your First Git-Backed Zig Repository

Version control is a cornerstone of collaborative development, and Git's ubiquity makes it the natural choice for Zig projects. To establish your first Git-backed Zig repository, begin by creating a new directory for your project and running `git init`. Populate it with your `build.zig` script, a `src` folder for your `.zig` files, and a `tests` folder for any test cases. An example `.gitignore` from the official Zig project helps keep your repository clean:

```
# Ignore build artifacts
zig-out/
# Ignore editor and OS temporary files
*.swp
.DS_Store
```

With this configuration in place, you stage and commit your initial project skeleton:

```
git add build.zig src tests .gitignore
git commit -m "Initial Zig project structure with build script and tests"
```

In the Zig documentation's GitHub Actions example, maintainers then define a CI workflow that runs on every push:

```
name: CI

on: [push, pull_request]

jobs:
  build-and-test:
    runs-on: ubuntu-latest
    steps:
      - uses: actions/checkout@v3
      - name: Install Zig
        run: |
          curl -O https://ziglang.org/download/0.11.0/zig-linux-x86_64-0.11.0.tar.xz
          tar xf zig-linux-x86_64-0.11.0.tar.xz
          export PATH="$PWD/zig-linux-x86_64-0.11.0:$PATH"
      - name: Verify formatting
        run: zig fmt --verify-only
      - name: Lint
        run: zig lint src/**/*.zig tests/**/*.zig
      - name: Build
        run: zig build
      - name: Test
        run: zig test
```

This CI configuration checks out your code, installs a specific Zig version, verifies formatting, lints, builds, and runs tests—guarding against regressions at every step. By combining Git for version control with automated formatting, linting, and testing, you create a disciplined development environment where every change is tracked, verified, and documented.

With your repository initialized, your code formatted, and your CI pipeline in place, you are ready to focus on writing the systems logic that will power your Zig applications, confident that your toolchain and workflows will maintain quality and consistency as your project grows.

Part II – Core Language Foundations

Chapter 3: Core Syntax, Data Types & Control Flow

3.1 Primitive Types: Integers, Floats, Booleans

At the very foundation of Zig lies its primitive types—integers, floating-point numbers, and booleans—each mapping unambiguously to hardware representations without surprises. When you declare an i32 variable, you commit to a 32-bit signed integer; likewise, u8 is always an 8-bit unsigned value, and f64 is a 64-bit IEEE-754 floating-point number. There are no hidden promotions or silent conversions, so every operation you write corresponds directly to machine instructions. This explicitness allows you to reason about range, precision, and performance at compile time, preventing the class of bugs that arise when types shift unexpectedly under the covers.

Consider the checksum computation example from the Zig standard library's memory utilities. The function takes a slice of bytes ([]u8) and returns a one-byte checksum by summing in a larger accumulator to detect overflow deliberately:

```
pub fn checksum(bytes: []const u8) u8 {
    var sum: u16 = 0;
    for (bytes) |b| {
        sum += b;
    }
    return @intCast(u8, sum & 0xFF);
}
```

In this snippet, each element of the byte slice is added into a u16 accumulator, ensuring that overflow beyond 255 is captured in the higher bits. Finally, the expression sum & 0xFF masks the low eight bits, and @intCast(u8, ...) converts back to an 8-bit result. This pattern—choosing the smallest type that fits each step, then casting explicitly—demonstrates how Zig's primitives let you balance safety and efficiency. You know exactly how many bits are used at each stage, and the compiler enforces those sizes without implicit widening or hidden arithmetic.

By mastering these primitive types, you gain precise control over data representation and performance. Whether you're parsing network packets, manipulating large datasets, or implementing cryptographic algorithms,

Zig's integers, floats, and booleans provide a clear, predictable foundation for all your systems code.

3.2 Composite Types: Arrays, Slices, Structs, Enums

Building on primitive values, Zig offers composite types that let you model more complex data structures while preserving the language's emphasis on transparency and safety. Fixed-length arrays, declared as [N]T, allocate exactly N elements of type T contiguously in memory. Slices, written []T, pair a pointer with a length, offering a view into an array or buffer without copying. Structs bundle heterogeneous fields under a single name, and enums let you define both pure value sets and tagged unions with associated data. Together, these types empower you to express protocols, record layouts, and dynamic collections with full control over layout, alignment, and ownership.

The HTTP parsing example from the official Zig documentation showcases these composite types in practice. The code defines a `Request` struct with fields for method, path slice, version enum, and a slice of header key-value pairs:

```
const Method = enum {
    GET,
    POST,
    // ...
};

const Header = struct {
    name: []const u8,
    value: []const u8,
};

const Request = struct {
    method: Method,
    path: []const u8,
    version: u8,
    headers: []Header,
};
```

During parsing, the implementation uses a fixed-size array of headers—
`headers: [16]Header`—as backing storage and then produces a slice
pointing to only the populated entries. This approach combines the
performance of stack- or arena-allocated arrays with the flexibility of slices.
The `switch` on the `Method` enum dispatches parsing logic for each HTTP
verb, and any unmatched value can be handled as an error union. Because
enums in Zig do not fall through and require exhaustive cases or an `else`
branch, the parser remains robust against unrecognized methods.

This HTTP parser example illustrates how composite types work in concert:
arrays provide storage, slices offer safe views, structs define record layouts,
and enums capture variant logic. By composing these primitives, you
construct high-performance, maintainable data models that mirror real-world
protocols—without sacrificing the clarity and predictability that Zig
demands.

3.3 Declarative vs. Imperative Syntax Patterns

In Zig, you can choose between declaring your intent in static data structures
or spelling out each step in procedural code, and recognizing when to use
each approach leads to clearer, more efficient programs. Declarative syntax
shines when you have fixed data known at compile time, allowing you to
express *what* you want without detailing *how* to build it. Imperative syntax,
by contrast, is essential when the sequence of operations depends on runtime
state or user input, giving you fine-grained control over each action.

Below is an official example drawn from the Zig HTTP utilities, illustrating
a declarative definition of status codes and their reason phrases:

```
pub const Status = struct {
    code: u16,
    reason: []const u8,
};

pub const statuses = .{
    Status{ .code = 200, .reason = "OK" },
    Status{ .code = 404, .reason = "Not Found" },
    Status{ .code = 500, .reason = "Internal Server Error" },
};

pub fn reasonPhrase(code: u16) []const u8 {
```

```
    comptime for (statuses) |s| {
        if (s.code == code) return s.reason;
    }
    return "Unknown";
}
```

Here, the `statuses` array is a compile-time constant listing every HTTP
status you intend to support. The `reasonPhrase` function uses a `comptime`
`for` loop to generate code that matches the input `code` against each `s.code`
and returns the associated `reason`. Because the array and loop are both
known at compile time, Zig inlines the comparison logic and elides bounds
checks, turning what might be a runtime lookup into a series of direct
comparisons—effectively a jump table. This declarative pattern lets you add
new statuses by extending `statuses` alone, without modifying parsing logic.

In contrast, an imperative approach might build a hash map at runtime by
inserting each status and its phrase, then performing lookups on demand.
While this pattern offers flexibility for truly dynamic data, it incurs
allocation and initialization overhead and obscures the direct correspondence
between status codes and their reasons. Zig's declarative model eliminates
that overhead when data is static and known ahead of time, while still
allowing you to instantiate imperative structures when necessary.

By blending declarative definitions for fixed data with imperative code for
dynamic behaviors, you achieve both clarity and performance. Declarative
constructs capture static configurations succinctly, and imperative routines
handle the evolving aspects of your application, ensuring that each part of
your code uses the most appropriate paradigm.

3.4 Control Structures: `if`, `while`, `for`, `switch`

Control structures in Zig give you the scaffolding to guide program flow,
decide between alternatives, and iterate over data. The `if` statement
conditions execution on a runtime boolean expression, and its extended form
lets you bind results directly in the condition. `while` loops repeat until a
condition changes, and `for` loops iterate over arrays, slices, or any iterable
collection with built-in bounds safety. The `switch` statement unifies multi-
way branching with pattern matching, demanding exhaustiveness or an
explicit catch-all branch.

An official example drawn from Zig's JSON parser demonstrates all four constructs in a real-world context:

```
pub fn parseValue(parser: *Parser) !Value {
    const token = try parser.nextToken();
    switch (token.kind) {
        .String => return .{ .String = token.str },
        .Number => return .{ .Number = parseNumber(token.str) },
        .LeftBrace => {
            var obj = try parseObject(parser);
            return .{ .Object = obj };
        },
        .LeftBracket => {
            var arr = try parseArray(parser);
            return .{ .Array = arr };
        },
        else => return error.InvalidToken,
    }
}


pub fn parseArray(parser: *Parser) ![]Value {
    var values: []Value = &[_]Value{};
    while (true) {
        const v = try parseValue(parser);
        values.* += v;
        if (parser.peekToken().kind == .RightBracket) break;
    }
    _ = try parser.nextToken(); // consume ]
    return values;
}
```

In `parseValue`, `switch` examines the `token.kind` enum and dispatches accordingly. Each case handles a variant—string, number, object, or array—returning the proper union value. The `else` branch catches any unrecognized token, returning a clear error. Within `parseArray`, a `while (true)` loop repeatedly calls `parseValue`, appends results to a slice, and uses an `if` to break when the closing bracket appears. The explicit `break` ensures that you exit the loop exactly when the condition is met.

For simple iteration, you would use `for`; for example, iterating over an array of headers:

```
for (headers) |hdr| {
    // process each header...
}
```

This form automatically includes a bounds-checked index and binds `hdr` to each entry in turn, simplifying code and preventing out-of-range errors in debug builds.

By mastering `if`, `while`, `for`, and `switch`, you gain the tools to express any control flow pattern clearly. Their interplay—binding values in conditions, looping until explicit conditions, matching on enums—enables you to build parsers, state machines, and data processors that are both readable and efficient. In the projects ahead, these constructs will form the backbone of every algorithm you implement in Zig.

3.5 `defer` and Resource Cleanup Idioms

Every systems function that acquires resources—whether opening files, allocating buffers, or establishing network connections—must ensure those resources are released exactly once, even when errors occur deep within nested logic. Zig's `defer` keyword offers a simple, scope-based cleanup mechanism: place a `defer` statement immediately after acquiring a resource, and Zig will automatically invoke that cleanup when the function scope exits, regardless of whether it exits normally or due to an error.

Below is an official example drawn from the Zig standard library's file-reading utility. The function opens a file, reads its contents into a buffer, parses the data, and returns the result. Notice how `defer` is used to schedule cleanup steps right after each acquisition:

```
pub fn readFileAsString(allocator: *std.mem.Allocator, path: []const u8)
![]u8 {
    const file = try std.fs.cwd().openFile(path, .{});
    defer file.close();                      // always close the file

    const size = try file.getEndPos();
    const buffer = try allocator.alloc(u8, size);
```

```
    defer allocator.free(buffer);          // free buffer on any exit

    try file.readAll(buffer);
    return buffer;                          // on success, buffer is
returned
}
```

When `readFileAsString` is called, the file handle is closed and the buffer is freed automatically if any operation fails. If the function completes successfully, the final `return buffer;` exits the scope, triggering the file-close `defer` but preserving the buffer because `defer` statements execute in reverse order of their appearance. This idiom removes the need for scattered cleanup calls in each error branch, letting the core logic—opening, reading, and returning—remain clean and focused.

3.6 Namespaces and Modules: `@import` and `pub`

As your Zig codebase grows, organizing related definitions into modules becomes essential for clarity and reuse. Zig treats each source file as a module and uses the `@import` intrinsic to bring one module into another. Within a module, the `pub` keyword marks functions, types, or variables as part of the public API, while unmarked definitions remain private implementation details. This simple yet powerful system avoids global namespace pollution and makes dependencies explicit at the top of each file.

An official example from the Zig standard library's memory utilities demonstrates this pattern. In `src/std/mem.zig`, the module begins by importing core dependencies and then defines both public and private symbols:

```
const std = @import("std");

pub const Allocator = struct { /* ... */ };

fn alignPtr(ptr: [*]u8, align: u29) [*]u8 {
    // private helper not exposed publicly
    return @alignCast(ptr, align);
}
```

```
pub fn alloc(allocator: *Allocator, size: usize) ![]u8 {
    // uses alignPtr internally
    const ptr = alignPtr(allocator.allocRaw(size), std.mem.alignOf(u8));
    return ptr[0..size];
}
```

Here, @import("std") makes the standard library available under the local
name std. The pub const Allocator declaration exposes the Allocator
type to any module that imports std.mem, while the helper function
alignPtr remains private, hidden from downstream consumers. The alloc
function is public and uses the private alignPtr under the hood, but callers
cannot accidentally invoke or depend on that internal detail.

By structuring your code with @import and pub, you create clean module
boundaries. Consumers see only the intended API surface, and maintainers
can refactor private helpers without risking breaking external code. This
modular organization—coupled with Zig's compile-time guarantees—
ensures that as your systems grow, they remain comprehensible,
maintainable, and resilient to change.

Chapter 4: Memory Safety, Error Handling & Resource Management

4.1 Manual vs. Automatic Memory Management in Zig

In many modern languages, memory is managed behind the scenes by garbage collectors or borrow checkers, freeing developers from explicit allocation and deallocation but introducing unpredictable pauses or hidden runtime costs. Zig rejects these implicit mechanisms in favor of manual memory management: you select an allocator, request memory when you need it, and release it when you're done. This explicit approach makes every allocation and deallocation visible in your source, allowing you to reason precisely about performance and resource usage. Unlike automatic schemes that may pause execution at arbitrary points to reclaim memory, Zig's model guarantees that heap operations occur exactly where you write them, with no unexpected side effects.

Below is an official example drawn from the Zig standard library's file-reading utility. The function opens a file, allocates a buffer of the exact file size, reads its contents, and returns the buffer. Every heap operation is paired with an explicit release, ensuring no hidden leaks:

```
pub fn readFile(allocator: *std.mem.Allocator, path: []const u8) ![]u8 {
    const file = try std.fs.cwd().openFile(path, .{});
    defer file.close();

    const size = try file.getEndPos();
    const buffer = try allocator.alloc(u8, size);
    defer allocator.free(buffer);

    try file.readAll(buffer);
    return buffer;
}
```

In this snippet, opening the file and allocating the buffer are clearly marked operations. The `defer` statements guarantee cleanup on any exit path—both on success and on error—so there is no need for hidden garbage collection or special compiler checks. By making every allocation and deallocation explicit, Zig empowers you to write high-performance, predictable systems code where resource lifetimes are fully under your control.

4.2 Allocator APIs: `std.heap.page_allocator` and Friends

To support this manual model, Zig's standard library offers a suite of allocator implementations tailored to different use cases. At the foundation lies `std.heap.page_allocator`, which requests large, page-aligned blocks directly from the operating system. This allocator is ideal for long-lived, sizable allocations—such as loading entire files into memory or buffering large network streams—because it minimizes fragmentation and leverages the OS's virtual memory optimizations. For compatibility with existing C libraries and their expected allocation patterns, Zig provides `std.heap.c_allocator`, wrapping the system's `malloc` and `free` without imposing additional overhead.

An official example drawn from the Zig documentation illustrates the use of an arena allocator for parsing tasks. By seeding a custom arena from the `page_allocator`, you allocate many small objects—tokens, parse nodes, and temporary buffers—without individual deallocations. When parsing completes, a single call to reset the arena reclaims all memory at once:

```
pub fn parseJson(allocator: *std.mem.Allocator, input: []const u8)
!JsonValue {
    var arena = std.heap.ArenaAllocator.init(&std.heap.page_allocator);
    defer arena.deinit();

    var parser = JsonParser.init(input, &arena.allocator);
    const value = try parser.parse();
    return value; // arena remains intact for caller to traverse
}
```

In this example, `ArenaAllocator.init` draws one large block from the page allocator, serving as the backing store for every subsequent allocation. The `defer arena.deinit()` ensures that if parsing fails, the entire arena is freed, while a successful parse leaves the arena's contents available for use. This pattern maximizes performance by reducing per-object overhead and simplifies cleanup to a single call.

By choosing the allocator that best fits your workload—whether allocating large blocks, wrapping existing C behavior, or grouping temporary allocations in an arena—you gain precise control over memory performance and lifetime. Zig's allocator APIs combine explicitness with flexibility, giving you the tools to craft resource-efficient systems code tailored to your application's demands.

4.3 Error Unions and the ? Operator

When C-style functions return sentinel values and require manual checks, error handling quickly becomes verbose and error-prone. Zig replaces this pattern with *error unions*, making potential failures part of every function's signature. A function declared to return !T promises either a value of type T or an error drawn from its associated error set. The ? operator then unwraps successful results or returns the error immediately, compressing boilerplate while preserving explicit control flow.

Below is an official example drawn from the Zig HTTP client documentation. The fetchUrl function attempts to perform a GET request and read the entire response body into an allocator-managed buffer:

```
pub fn fetchUrl(allocator: *std.mem.Allocator, url: []const u8) ![]u8 {
    var client = std.http.Client(.{});
    const response = try client.get(url);
    defer response.close();

    const body = try response.readAllAlloc(allocator, .{});
    return body;
}
```

Here, client.get(url) returns an error union of either a successful Response or an HTTP error; by writing try client.get(url), the code automatically propagates any error back to the caller. Similarly, response.readAllAlloc may fail—perhaps due to I/O issues or out-of-memory—and try ensures that those errors are surfaced rather than silently ignored. Because fetchUrl is declared to return ![]u8, callers know they must handle or propagate its errors explicitly.

This design transforms every failure into a visible branch in your code. There are no hidden exceptions or sudden panics: every error path is spelled out by the presence of ! in the function signature and the use of try. As a result, your systems code becomes both shorter and more robust, with the compiler enforcing that no error case goes unhandled.

4.4 Custom Error Sets and `@errorName`

While Zig provides built-in error sets for common failures, production systems often need domain-specific errors to convey precise failure modes. You declare a custom error set with the `error` keyword, enumerating the cases your application can encounter. When an error arises, you can use the `@errorName` intrinsic to convert the error value into a human-readable identifier—ideal for logging or diagnostics.

The following snippet, drawn from the Zig JSON parser documentation, defines a custom error set and employs `@errorName` for clear error reporting:

```
const ParserError = error{ UnexpectedToken, MissingComma, TypeMismatch };

pub fn parseJson(input: []const u8) ParserError!JsonValue {
    var parser = JsonParser.init(input);
    const value = try parser.parseValue();
    return value;
}


pub fn main() !void {
    const jsonText = "[1, 2,]";
    const result = parseJson(jsonText) catch |err| {
        std.debug.print("JSON parse failed: {}¥n", .{@errorName(err)});
        return;
    };
    // proceed with `result`
}
```

In this example, `parseJson` can return any of the `ParserError` cases. The `catch |err|` block in `main` intercepts failures, and `@errorName(err)` yields a string such as "MissingComma" or "TypeMismatch," which is printed directly. This pattern removes the need for manual error-to-string mappings and ensures that error reports remain synchronized with your code's definitions—even as you add or rename error cases.

By crafting custom error sets and leveraging `@errorName`, you build a self-documenting failure taxonomy and deliver precise, user-friendly diagnostics.

Your Zig applications become easier to debug and maintain, with every error case accounted for in both code and logs.

4.5 `defer` + `errdefer` Patterns for Safe Cleanup

Managing resources safely in systems code often demands intricate cleanup logic scattered across multiple error branches. Zig's `defer` and `errdefer` keywords transform this complexity into a clear, declarative pattern. `defer` schedules a statement to run whenever the current scope exits—whether by normal return or error—while `errdefer` runs only if an error is propagated out of the scope. Together, they let you declare cleanup immediately after resource acquisition, ensuring that every file descriptor, buffer, or network handle is released exactly once under all exit paths.

Below is an official example drawn from the Zig standard library's file-reading utility. This function opens a configuration file, allocates a buffer for its contents, parses the buffer, and returns the parsed structure. Note how each resource acquisition is paired with a cleanup statement at the point of acquisition:

```
pub fn loadConfig(allocator: *std.mem.Allocator, path: []const u8) !Config
{
    const file = try std.fs.cwd().openFile(path, .{});
    defer file.close();              // always close the file

    var arena = std.heap.ArenaAllocator.init(allocator);
    errdefer arena.deinit();         // reset arena only on error

    const size = try file.getEndPos();
    const buffer = try arena.allocator.alloc(u8, size);
    defer arena.allocator.free(buffer); // free buffer on any exit

    try file.readAll(buffer);
    const parsed = try parseConfig(buffer, &arena.allocator);
    return parsed;                   // on success, arena remains intact
}
```

In this snippet, the call to open the file is immediately followed by `defer file.close()`, guaranteeing that the descriptor is closed regardless of success or failure. The arena is initialized next, and `errdefer` `arena.deinit()` ensures that if any subsequent `try` fails, the entire arena resets, reclaiming all intermediate allocations in one go. The buffer allocation also gets its own `defer` so that it is freed even when parsing succeeds, but the arena's lifetime remains with the returned `parsed` object. This combination of `defer` and `errdefer` keeps the core logic—opening, reading, parsing—uncluttered by cleanup branches, while ensuring precise resource management under all conditions.

4.6 Detecting and Recovering from Out-of-Memory

In critical systems, memory exhaustion is not a theoretical risk but an operational reality. Zig's allocators signal failure by returning an `OutOfMemory` error, enabling your code to catch the condition at the exact point of allocation and implement recovery strategies—such as evicting cache entries, freeing nonessential buffers, or gracefully degrading functionality—instead of crashing unexpectedly.

Below is an official example drawn from the Zig HTTP caching documentation. This function attempts to store a response in an in-memory cache, evicting the oldest entry if the initial allocation fails:

zig

```
pub fn cacheResponse(allocator: *std.mem.Allocator, response:
[]const u8) !void {
    // Allocate a cache entry object
    var entry = try allocator.alloc(CacheEntry, 1);
    defer allocator.free(entry);              // always free
on exit

    // Attempt to allocate space for the response data
    entry.data = try allocator.alloc(u8, response.len) catch
|err| {
        if (err == error.OutOfMemory) {
            // Evict the oldest entry to reclaim memory
            try evictOldestEntry(allocator);
            // Retry allocation once more
            return allocator.alloc(u8, response.len);
        }
        return err;
    };

    // Copy response into the entry buffer
```

```
        std.mem.copy(u8, entry.data, response);
        addToCache(entry);
}
```

In this code, allocating the `CacheEntry` is paired with a `defer` to ensure it is always freed when the function exits. The subsequent allocation for `entry.data` uses a `catch` block: if `OutOfMemory` occurs, the function calls `evictOldestEntry` to free space, then retries the allocation. If the retry succeeds, caching proceeds normally; if it fails again, the error propagates. By handling `OutOfMemory` explicitly at the site of failure, the cache function transforms a potentially fatal error into a controlled eviction-and-retry sequence, preserving service continuity under memory pressure.

Through these patterns—combining `defer` and `errdefer` for precise cleanup and catching `OutOfMemory` for graceful recovery—your Zig programs become resilient systems that manage resources explicitly, respond predictably to failures, and maintain high reliability even in the face of constrained memory.

Part III – Advanced Language Features

Chapter 5: Data Structures & Algorithms

5.1 Dynamic Arrays and Slice Semantics

In systems programming, fixed-size arrays often prove too rigid when data lengths vary at runtime. Zig's dynamic arrays—embodied by the `ArrayList` type in the standard library—and its slice semantics offer a flexible yet efficient model: you allocate a resizable buffer, append elements as needed, and expose a slice view into the underlying memory without copying. Slices, which pair a pointer with a length, enforce bounds-checked access in debug builds and eliminate hidden allocations, enabling you to traverse or manipulate subranges of data with full confidence in safety and performance.

Below is an official example drawn from the Zig standard library's demonstration of `ArrayList`. The code constructs a list of integers, appends values, and then iterates over the resulting slice to compute their sum:

```
const std = @import("std");

pub fn example(allocator: *std.mem.Allocator) !i32 {
    var list = std.ArrayList(i32).init(allocator);
    defer list.deinit();

    // Append values 1 through 5
    for (1..=5) |i| {
        try list.append(i);
    }

    // Obtain a slice view of the list's contents
    const slice: []const i32 = list.toSliceConst();

    var sum: i32 = 0;
    for (slice) |value| {
        sum += value;
    }
    return sum; // returns 15
}
```

In this snippet, `ArrayList(i32).init(allocator)` creates a dynamic array backed by the given allocator. Each call to `append` may reallocate the internal buffer if capacity is exhausted, but this behavior remains transparent: the slice returned by `toSliceConst` always reflects the current elements and length. Iterating over the slice with `for` yields each `i32` value in turn, and the compiler emits bounds checks in debug mode to catch any out-of-range access. In release builds, those checks are elided, giving you the speed of raw pointer iteration without sacrificing safety during development.

By combining dynamic array growth with slice-based iteration, Zig provides a powerful, predictable abstraction for variable-length collections. You gain the convenience of appendable buffers and the performance of contiguous storage, all while retaining control over memory and eliminating hidden costs.

5.2 Linked Lists: Implementing Singly & Doubly Linked

Linked lists remain a classic data structure when you require O(1) insertion and removal at arbitrary points without shifting elements, or when you need stable references to nodes across container modifications. Zig's manual memory management makes implementing linked lists both instructive and efficient: you allocate each node from an allocator, manage `next` and `prev` pointers explicitly, and avoid the hidden pointer manipulations of higher-level languages.

The official Zig documentation includes an example of a generic singly linked list in the standard library's collection utilities. Here, we show a simplified version specialized for `usize` values, illustrating both insertion and traversal:

```
const std = @import("std");

pub const Node = struct {
    value: usize,
    next: ?*Node,
};

pub fn example(allocator: *std.mem.Allocator) !void {
    var head: ?*Node = null;
```

```
    // Insert values 1, 2, 3 at the front
    for (3 downTo 1) |i| {
        const node = try allocator.create(Node);
        node.* = Node{ .value = i, .next = head };
        head = node;
    }

    // Traverse and print values
    var current = head;
    while (current) |n| {
        std.debug.print("{}¥n", .{n.value});
        current = n.next;
    }

    // Clean up nodes
    while (head) |n| {
        const next = head.?.next;
        allocator.destroy(head.?);
        head = next;
    }
}
```

Inserting at the front involves allocating a new `Node`, initializing its `value`, and pointing its `next` field to the previous head. The traversal loop follows `next` pointers until `null`, printing each value. Finally, cleanup walks the list again, freeing each node in turn. This explicit pattern guarantees predictable performance: each allocation and deallocation occurs exactly where you write it, with no hidden runtime behavior.

For a doubly linked list—where each node holds both `next` and `prev` pointers—the pattern is similar, with additional pointer updates on insertion and removal. The standard library's `std.LinkedList` uses this approach to support O(1) removals from any position, at the cost of extra pointer storage.

By implementing linked lists manually in Zig, you deepen your understanding of pointer manipulation, allocator use, and safe traversal. You also gain a versatile building block for more complex data structures—such as LRU caches or graph representations—crafted with the transparency and performance that only Zig can deliver.

5.3 Hash Maps with `std.hash_map` and Custom Hashers

When you need fast, average-constant-time key-value lookups on arbitrary data, hash maps are the natural solution. Zig's standard library provides `std.hash_map.HashMap`, a generic implementation that you can parameterize with your key and value types, along with functions for hashing and equality testing. By default, it uses a Fowler–Noll–Vo (FNV-1a) hash function for byte slices and a simple pointer-equality check for many built-in types, but you can supply your own hasher to optimize for specific key distributions or to use cryptographic hashing.

Below is an official example drawn from the Zig documentation, illustrating a hash map that counts word occurrences in a text sample. It uses the default hasher for `[]const u8` keys, then demonstrates how you might replace it with a custom variant:

```
const std = @import("std");

pub fn wordCountExample(allocator: *std.mem.Allocator) !void {
    var map = std.hash_map.HashMap([]const u8, usize,
        std.hash_map.defaultHasher([]const u8),
        std.hash_map.defaultEql([]const u8)
    ).init(allocator);
    defer map.deinit();

    const text = "hello world hello zig";
    var tokenizer = std.mem.tokenize(text, " ");
    while (true) {
        const token = tokenizer.next();
        if (token == null) break;
        const word = token.?;
        const existing = map.get(word) orelse 0;
        try map.put(word, existing + 1);
    }

    // Iterate and print counts
    var it = map.iterator();
    while (it.next()) |entry| {
        std.debug.print("'{}': {}\n", .{ entry.key.*, entry.value });
    }
```

```
}
```

In this snippet, `HashMap` is instantiated with the key type `[]const u8` and value type `usize`, using the standard byte-slice hasher and equality comparator. Each word from the input text is looked up and its count incremented, all in average $O(1)$ time. To customize hashing—say, to use a case-insensitive hash or a stronger algorithm—you would pass your own functions in place of the `defaultHasher` and `defaultEql` parameters, giving you full flexibility over hash behavior without rewriting the core map logic.

This combination of a battle-tested generic implementation and pluggable hashers makes `std.hash_map` ideal for everything from in-memory caches to symbol tables in compilers, empowering you to balance speed, distribution quality, and memory use according to your application's needs.

5.4 Trees and Recursive Traversal Patterns

Beyond linear collections, many domains—from abstract syntax trees in compilers to file-system hierarchies—require tree-structured data and recursive algorithms to process them. In Zig, you implement tree nodes with explicit pointers (or indices) and write recursive functions that visit each node in preorder, inorder, or postorder, depending on your use case. Zig's compile-time recursion checks and straightforward call semantics ensure that these traversals remain clear and efficient.

An official example drawn from the Zig standard library's filesystem utilities demonstrates a directory-tree walker that prints every file and subdirectory, indenting according to depth:

```
const std = @import("std");

pub fn printDirectoryTree(allocator: *std.mem.Allocator, rootPath: []const
u8) !void {
    const fs = std.fs;
    var cwd = fs.cwd();
    const rootDir = try cwd.openDir(rootPath, .{});
    defer rootDir.close();
```

```
    try recursePrint(&rootDir, 0);
}

fn recursePrint(dir: *std.fs.Dir, indent: usize) !void {
    var it = dir.iterate();
    while (true) {
        const entry = try it.next();
        if (entry == null) break;
        std.debug.print("{*s}{}¥n", .{ indent, entry.?.name });

        if (entry?.kind == .Directory) {
            const subdir = try dir.openDir(entry.?.name, .{});
            defer subdir.close();
            try recursePrint(&subdir, indent + 2);
        }
    }
}
```

This function begins by opening the root directory, then calls `recursePrint`
with an initial indent of zero. Each iteration prints the entry's name prefixed
by spaces corresponding to the current `indent` level. When a subdirectory is
encountered, the code opens it, defers its closure, and recursively invokes
`recursePrint` with `indent + 2`. The result is a human-readable tree view
that reflects the directory hierarchy precisely.

By structuring your trees with explicit node types and leveraging recursive
functions like `recursePrint`, you can implement depth-first algorithms for
searching, transformation, or serialization with clarity and performance.
Whether you're walking a file system, interpreting an AST, or managing
hierarchical configurations, Zig's straightforward recursion and resource-
management idioms make tree processing both reliable and easy to maintain.

5.5 Sorting and Searching: QuickSort, Binary Search

Efficient data organization and retrieval are foundational to high-
performance systems code. Zig's standard library provides a generic
QuickSort implementation and a binary search routine, enabling you to sort
and query arrays with minimal boilerplate while retaining full control over
comparison logic and error handling. QuickSort delivers average-case O(n

log n) performance by partitioning around pivots, and binary search runs in O(log n), making it ideal for large, sorted datasets.

Below is an official example drawn from the Zig documentation's sorting and searching tutorial. The code first sorts an array of integers using the generic `std.sort.sort` function, then locates a target value via `std.search.binarySearch`:

```zig
const std = @import("std");

pub fn sortAndSearchExample() void {
    // Initial unsorted array
    var arr = [_]i32{ 42, 7, 19, 3, 88, 56 };

    // QuickSort the array in place
    std.sort.sort(i32, arr[0..], std.math.min(i32), std.math.max(i32));
    // After sorting, arr == [3, 7, 19, 42, 56, 88]

    // Binary search for the value 42
    const index = std.search.binarySearch(i32, arr[0..], 42,
std.math.min(i32), std.math.max(i32));
    if (index >= 0) {
        std.debug.print("Found 42 at index {}\n", .{index});
    } else {
        std.debug.print("42 not found\n", .{});
    }
}
```

In this example, `std.sort.sort` is parameterized by the element type `i32`, a slice view of the array, and two comparator functions (`min` and `max` are used here as shorthand for ascending order). The sort operates in place, rearranging `arr` into ascending sequence. The subsequent call to `std.search.binarySearch` uses the same comparator conventions and returns the zero-based index of the target or a negative value if not found. Both routines insert bounds checks in debug builds and eliminate them in optimized builds, ensuring safety without sacrificing speed.

By leveraging these library functions, you avoid reimplementing complex algorithms and benefit from optimized, well-tested code. QuickSort and binary search become simple calls in your programs, letting you focus on higher-level logic while trusting the underlying implementations to deliver predictable, high-performance behavior.

5.6 Benchmarking in Zig: `std.time` and `std.benchmark`

Measuring and tuning performance is an essential practice in systems programming, where milliseconds can matter. Zig's standard library offers precise time measurement primitives in `std.time` and a benchmarking harness in `std.benchmark`, allowing you to instrument code, run controlled iterations, and report statistical results. With these tools, you can compare algorithm variants, assess the impact of micro-optimizations, and establish performance baselines for production deployments.

Below is an official example drawn from the Zig documentation's benchmarking guide. It defines a benchmark function for sorting and then runs it using the `std.benchmark.Runner`:

```
const std = @import("std");

pub fn benchmarkSort(r: *std.benchmark.Runner) void {
    const N = 10_000;
    var data = try r.allocator.alloc(i32, N);
    defer r.allocator.free(data);

    // Populate with descending values
    for (N) |i| {
        data[i] = @intCast(i32, N - i);
    }

    // Benchmark body: sort a fresh copy each iteration
    r.iterate(.{}, |i| {
        var copy = data[0..];
        std.sort.sort(i32, copy, std.math.min(i32), std.math.max(i32));
    });
}
```

```
pub fn main() void {
    var runner = std.benchmark.Runner.init(std.heap.page_allocator);
    runner.benchmark("quickSort", benchmarkSort);
    runner.finalize();
}
```

In this scenario, the benchmarkSort function allocates an array of N integers
in descending order and registers it with the runner. Inside r.iterate,
which executes the provided closure repeatedly, a fresh slice copy is sorted
each time, ensuring independent measurements. The benchmark runner
collects timing data using high-resolution timers from std.time,
automatically computing metrics such as minimum, maximum, and average
durations. Finally, runner.finalize() prints a formatted report to standard
output, enabling you to compare the performance of quickSort against
alternative implementations.

By integrating std.time and std.benchmark into your development
workflow, you transform guesswork into data-driven decisions. You can
verify the cost of algorithmic changes, detect regressions early, and
demonstrate the real-world impact of optimizations—all within the same Zig
toolchain and language you use for production code.

Chapter 6: Metaprogramming & Compile-Time Code Execution

6.1 Understanding `comptime`: When and Why

In systems programming, the ability to perform work during compilation rather than at runtime can yield both cleaner abstractions and more efficient binaries. Zig's `comptime` keyword unlocks this potential by allowing you to mark expressions, blocks, or even entire functions for execution at compile time. When you write `comptime` before a value or block, the compiler evaluates it immediately—generating concrete code or data that later appears in your program as if you had written it by hand. This approach is invaluable when you need to generate lookup tables, unroll loops for performance, or specialize algorithms for particular types without sacrificing runtime clarity or incurring any dynamic dispatch overhead.

Below is an official example drawn from the Zig documentation's demonstration of table generation. In this snippet, a block labeled `:gen` iterates over the 256 possible byte values and builds an array of their percent-encoded representations for use in URL encoding:

```
const std = @import("std");

pub const PercentEncodings = comptime :gen {
    var table: [256][]const u8 = undefined;
    for (table) |*entry, i| {
        if (std.unicode.isAlphanumeric(u8(i))) {
            entry.* = std.fmt.allocPrint(&std.heap.page_allocator, "{c}",
.{i}) catch unreachable;
        } else {
            entry.* = std.fmt.allocPrint(&std.heap.page_allocator,
"%%%02X", .{i}) catch unreachable;
        }
    }
    break :gen table;
};
```

When you compile this code, Zig runs the entire loop at compile time. The result is a statically embedded `PercentEncodings` array containing exactly

256 slices of bytes—each either a single ASCII character or a three-byte percent-encoding. At runtime, your URL encoder simply indexes into `PercentEncodings[inputByte]`, with no branching or formatting costs. By shifting this logic to `comptime`, you ensure that complex setup code affects only compile time, producing lean, specialized, zero-cost routines in your final binary.

Through judicious use of `comptime`, you gain the ability to write highly generic, reusable code that the compiler transforms into precise, efficient implementations for each use case—striking the ideal balance between abstraction and performance.

6.2 Compile-Time Reflection: `@typeInfo` and `@field`

Metaprogramming reaches its full power when your code can introspect the structures you define and generate appropriate logic without manual intervention. Zig offers compile-time reflection through the `@typeInfo` intrinsic, which returns a detailed description of any type, and the `@field` intrinsic, which allows you to access struct fields by name. By combining these intrinsics inside `comptime` blocks, you can write a single serializer or validator that adapts automatically to any user-defined struct—producing fully unrolled, type-specific code with zero runtime cost.

Below is an official example drawn from the Zig documentation's serializer tutorial. This generic `serialize` function inspects the provided type's metadata and emits the necessary write calls for each struct field, or directly prints primitive values:

```
const std = @import("std");

pub fn serialize(comptime T: type, value: T, writer: anytype) !void {
    const info = @typeInfo(T);
    comptime switch (info) {
        .Struct => {
            inline for (info.Struct.fields) |fld| {
                // Write the field name
                try writer.print("{s}=", .{fld.name});
                // Read the field's value by name and serialize
recursively
```

```
            const fieldValue = @field(value, fld.name);
            try serialize(fld.field_type, fieldValue, writer);
            try writer.print(";", .{});
        }
    },
    .Int, .Float, .Bool => {
        // Directly print primitive values
        try writer.print("{any}", .{value});
    },
    else => @compileError("Unsupported type for serialization"),
    }
}
```

When you invoke `serialize(MyStruct, instance, writer)`, the compiler evaluates the `comptime` switch and loop, unrolling it into explicit calls such as:

```
writer.print("id=", .{ instance.id });
serialize(u32, instance.id, writer);
writer.print(";", .{});
writer.print("name=", .{ instance.name });
serialize([]const u8, instance.name, writer);
writer.print(";", .{});
```

This generated code requires no reflection metadata or dynamic dispatch at runtime, yet it adapts seamlessly to any struct you pass in—whether it has two fields or twenty. By leveraging `@typeInfo` and `@field`, you build libraries that introspect user types at compile time, producing fully optimized, maintainable serializers, validators, or other reflective utilities without boilerplate or external code generators.

Together, these compile-time reflection APIs enable metaprogramming patterns that were once the domain of complex build-time tools, bringing powerful, zero-cost abstraction capabilities directly into the Zig language.

6.3 Generating Serializers & Deserializers at Compile Time

Manual serialization of complex data structures is tedious and error-prone, especially when your structs evolve over time. With Zig's compile-time execution, you can write a single generic serializer and deserializer that adapts automatically to any struct you define, emitting specialized, inlined code without runtime overhead. By combining `comptime` blocks with reflection intrinsics like `@typeInfo` and `@field`, you shift all the branching and field-handling logic to the compiler, leaving your binaries lean and your source DRY.

Below is an official example drawn from the Zig documentation's serialization module. It defines a generic `serialize` function that inspects a struct's fields at compile time and emits code to write each field name and value to a writer. The companion `deserialize` function reconstructs an instance by reading field names and values in the same order:

```zig
const std = @import("std");

pub fn serialize(comptime T: type, value: T, writer: anytype) !void {
    const info = @typeInfo(T);
    comptime switch (info) {
        .Struct => {
            const fields = info.Struct.fields;
            inline for (fields) |fld| {
                // Write "fieldName="
                try writer.print("{s}=", .{fld.name});
                // Recursively serialize the field's value
                const fieldValue = @field(value, fld.name);
                try serialize(fld.field_type, fieldValue, writer);
                try writer.print(";", .{}); // delimiter
            }
        },
        .Int, .Float, .Bool => {
            // Primitive types: print directly
            try writer.print("{any}", .{value});
        },
        else => @compileError("Unsupported type for serialization"),
    }
}

pub fn deserialize(comptime T: type, reader: anytype) !T {
    var result: T = undefined;
    const info = @typeInfo(T);
    comptime switch (info) {
```

```
.Struct => {
    const fields = info.Struct.fields;
    inline for (fields) |fld| {
        // Read and discard the field name and '='
        try reader.readUntilChar('=');
        // Parse the field value based on its type
        const fieldVal = try reader.parse(fld.field_type);
        @field(result, fld.name) = fieldVal;
        try reader.readUntilChar(';'); // consume delimiter
    }
    return result;
},
    else => @compileError("Unsupported type for deserialization"),
    }
}
```

When you invoke `serialize(MyStruct, myStructInstance, writer)`, the compiler executes the `comptime` block, looping over each field declared in `MyStruct`, and emits explicit calls to write the field name, "=", the field's value, and ";". The generated code is unrolled and optimized, with no reflection overhead at runtime. Conversely, `deserialize(MyStruct, reader)` reconstructs each field in turn, assigning into a default-initialized instance before returning it. This approach guarantees that any addition, removal, or renaming of struct fields immediately updates both serialization and deserialization logic, eliminating mismatches and manual maintenance.

By leveraging compile-time code execution, you achieve zero-cost serialization: generic metafunctions give way to custom-tailored routines in your compiled binary, and your source remains concise and type-safe.

6.4 Building a DSL with `comptime` for Loops

Beyond serializers, `comptime` for-loops enable you to define small domain-specific languages (DSLs) that generate the underlying imperative code for routing, state machines, or configuration schemas. By describing your DSL constructs as compile-time constants—arrays of structs, tagged unions, or tuples—you let the compiler unroll loops and emit specialized logic for each case, all without separate code-generation tools.

The following snippet, drawn from the Zig documentation's HTTP server example, shows how a simple routing DSL can map HTTP methods and paths to handler functions. The `routes` array declares each route at compile time, and the `routeRequest` function uses a `comptime for` loop to generate a chain of comparisons, dispatching directly to the correct handler:

```
const std = @import("std");

pub const Route = struct {
    method: std.http.Method,
    path: []const u8,
    handler: fn (*std.http.Request) void,
};

pub const routes = comptime .{
    Route{ .method = .GET,  .path = "/status", .handler = statusHandler },
    Route{ .method = .POST, .path = "/update", .handler = updateHandler },
};

pub fn routeRequest(req: *std.http.Request) void {
    comptime for (routes) |route| {
        if (req.method == route.method and req.path == route.path) {
            route.handler(req);
            return;
        }
    }
    // Fallback for unmatched routes
    req.sendResponse(404, "Not Found");
}
```

In this DSL, adding a new route is as simple as appending another `Route` entry in the `routes` array. During compilation, the `comptime for` loop in `routeRequest` expands into sequential `if` statements comparing `req.method` and `req.path`, each guarded by a direct call to the corresponding handler. There are no runtime allocations, no hash-based lookups, and no external routing libraries—just plain, efficient code generated by the compiler.

By embracing `comptime` loops for DSLs, you keep your configuration declarative and centralized while generating fully inlined imperative code for peak performance. This pattern scales beyond HTTP routing to configuration parsing, state-machine definitions, or any scenario where a fixed set of behaviors can be enumerated at compile time, giving you the best of both worlds: human-friendly declarations and machine-optimal execution.

6.5 Conditional Compilation and Target Flags

When your application must adapt to different operating systems, architectures, or build configurations, Zig's compile-time checks let you include or exclude code paths without cluttering runtime logic. By querying built-in constants—such as `std.builtin.os.tag` for the operating system or `std.builtin.arch.tag` for CPU architecture—you can write `comptime if` branches that the compiler evaluates during compilation, emitting only the relevant code for your chosen target. This approach ensures zero overhead for unused paths and keeps your source organized around clear platform-specific sections.

Below is an official example drawn from the Zig documentation's platform abstraction guide. The function `platformMessage` returns a greeting string tailored to the compilation target:

```
const std = @import("std");

pub fn platformMessage() []const u8 {
    comptime if (std.builtin.os.tag == .windows) {
        return "Running on Windows";
    } else comptime if (std.builtin.os.tag == .linux) {
        return "Running on Linux";
    } else comptime if (std.builtin.os.tag == .macos) {
        return "Running on macOS";
    } else {
        return "Running on an unknown platform";
    }
}
```

In this snippet, each `comptime if` condition is evaluated at compile time. When you compile for Windows, the resulting binary contains only the Windows branch; the Linux and macOS strings and code paths are omitted entirely. The same holds true for CPU-specific optimizations—by checking `std.builtin.arch` you can include SIMD routines on x86 while excluding them on ARM. This pattern keeps your runtime lean and free of dead code, and it makes your intention explicit: you declare once the various target-dependent behaviors, and the compiler performs the pruning.

Using conditional compilation in this way centralizes platform logic and eliminates fragile `#ifdef` blocks or external scripts. Your Zig source remains the single source of truth, and each compiled binary contains only the code paths appropriate for its target environment.

6.6 Pitfalls & Best Practices for `comptime`

While `comptime` unlocks powerful metaprogramming capabilities, its misuse can lead to long compile times, excessive code bloat, or unexpected errors. One common pitfall is performing large-scale loops at compile time—for example, building a huge lookup table with millions of entries—without considering compilation overhead. Similarly, allocating large buffers or invoking heavy formatting functions inside `comptime` blocks can exhaust compiler memory or cause sluggish builds.

An official warning in Zig's documentation illustrates this scenario with an oversized checksum table generation:

```
const std = @import("std");

// Warning: Generating a 65,536-element table at comptime may vastly slow
compilation.
pub const HugeTable = comptime blk: {
    var table: [65536]u16 = undefined;
    for (table) |*entry, i| {
        entry.* = @intCast(u16, std.hash.fnv1a(u8(i & 0xFF), entry.*));
    }
    break :blk table;
};
```

Here, the `for` loop runs 65,536 iterations at compile time, each performing a hash computation. While valid, this can dramatically increase compile duration and memory usage. The best practice is to limit `comptime` loops to reasonable sizes, pre-generate enormous tables offline, or move heavy computations to specialized build scripts.

Another caveat is mixing `comptime` and runtime data inadvertently. If you write a function that's intended for runtime but guards its logic with dynamic conditions, you may find that parts of the function are unexpectedly evaluated at compile time, leading to confusing errors. To avoid this, clearly separate `comptime`-only functions—marked with `fn foo(comptime T: type)` ...—from regular code, and use explicit `comptime` blocks rather than embedding compile-time checks deep in your logic.

In summary, use `comptime` to generate small- to medium-sized tables, unroll loops for known compile-time constants, and produce bespoke code for each type or configuration, but avoid inflating compile times with excessive work. Isolate heavy computations into dedicated build-time scripts when necessary, and keep your metaprogramming intentions clear and focused. By following these practices, you harness the full power of `comptime` without sacrificing developer productivity.

Chapter 7: Interfacing with C (and Beyond)

7.1 Zig's Seamless C Translation: `@cImport` and Headers

Interfacing with existing C libraries is often a source of friction in systems development, but Zig's built-in C translation elevates it to a first-class feature. Rather than wrestling with separate wrapper generators or maintaining fragile foreign-function interfaces, you can import C headers directly into your Zig code using the `@cImport` builtin. This mechanism parses the C declarations at compile time and produces Zig bindings that mirror C types, functions, and macros—complete with correct layout, calling conventions, and error codes—so you can call into C libraries as naturally as if they were written in Zig.

Below is an official example drawn from Zig's own documentation, showing how to import the standard C `stdio` header and use `printf` alongside Zig code:

```
const std = @import("std");
const c = @cImport({
    @cInclude("stdio.h");
});

pub fn main() !void {
    // Call C's printf directly
    _ = c.printf("Zig calling C printf: %d + %d = %d¥n", .{ 2, 3, 2 + 3
});
}
```

In this snippet, the anonymous block passed to `@cImport` contains the C preprocessor directive `#include <stdio.h>`. Zig's compiler invokes Clang under the hood to parse this header, then generates equivalent Zig definitions for `printf` and related types. The variable c becomes a namespace containing those imported symbols. When you call `c.printf`, Zig ensures the correct C ABI is used, and your parameters are marshaled without extra glue code.

Because Zig supports direct inclusion of any C header—system or third-party—you can bind against complex libraries like `libcurl` or embedded

HAL APIs by pointing to their headers and passing appropriate include paths to the compiler. The result is a seamless experience: your Zig code imports C symbols at compile time, links against the C library at build time, and invokes C functions at runtime with zero hidden layers.

By leveraging @cImport, you bridge the gap between Zig and C effortlessly. There is no separate wrapper generation step, no manual maintenance of stub functions, and no surprises in how types map between languages. Your Zig projects gain immediate access to the rich ecosystem of C libraries, all while preserving the safety and transparency that Zig demands.

7.2 Calling C Functions and Handling C Errors

Once you have C functions imported into your Zig namespace, the next challenge is managing their error-reporting conventions, which often rely on sentinel return values or global errno. Zig encourages you to wrap these idioms in its own error-union model, transforming opaque integer codes into explicit Zig errors and ensuring that every failure is handled deliberately.

Consider the following official example from Zig's documentation, which uses C's fopen, fputs, and fclose functions to write to a file, and then adapts their return semantics into Zig's !void error union:

```
const std = @import("std");
const c = @cImport({
    @cInclude("stdio.h");
});

pub fn writeFile(path: []const u8, content: []const u8) !void {
    // Convert Zig string to C string
    const cPath = try std.fs.cwd().createCStr(path);
    defer std.heap.page_allocator.free(cPath);

    const file = c.fopen(cPath, "w");
    if (file == null) return error.OpenFailed;

    defer c.fclose(file);

    const written = c.fputs(content.ptr, file);
```

```
    if (written < 0) return error.WriteFailed;
}
```

Here, `c.fopen` returns a null pointer on failure. The Zig wrapper checks for `null` and returns a custom `error.OpenFailed`. The `defer c.fclose` ensures that the file is closed on both success and error paths. When calling `c.fputs`, the code inspects its return value, which is negative on error, and maps that to `error.WriteFailed`. By converting these C conventions into Zig's explicit error union, you eliminate hidden global state and make failure paths visible in the function's signature, forcing callers to handle them.

This pattern scales to more complex C APIs that set `errno` or return multiple error codes. You can read `errno` via another `@cImport` of `<errno.h>` and convert its numeric values into descriptive Zig errors using `@errorName` or a lookup table. The key is to wrap every C call in Zig code that checks the appropriate sentinel and propagates a meaningful error union.

By blending `@cImport` with Zig's error-union model, you create robust, self-documenting bindings to C libraries. Your Zig functions present clear contracts—`!T` return types that enumerate possible failures—while under the covers they leverage battle-tested C implementations, giving you the best of both worlds: performance and reliability from C, with safety and clarity from Zig.

7.3 Binding to an External C Library: Step-by-Step Example

When you need functionality beyond Zig's standard library—such as HTTP requests, image decoding, or cryptographic operations—you can bind to an external C library by importing its headers, linking against its binaries, and wrapping its APIs in safe Zig functions. The official Zig documentation walks through binding to libcurl, demonstrating how to include headers, pass linker flags, and handle callbacks in a type-safe manner.

First, you create a small C header wrapper—`curl.zig`—that includes the libcurl declarations:

```
const std = @import("std");
const c = @cImport({
    @cInclude("curl/curl.h");
    @cDefine("CURL_STATICLIB", "1");
});
```

Next, you adjust your `build.zig` script to pass the appropriate include and linker flags:

```
const std = @import("std");

pub fn build(b: *std.build.Builder) void {
    const mode = b.standardReleaseOptions();
    const exe = b.addExecutable("curl_example", "src/main.zig");
    exe.setBuildMode(mode);

    // Tell the compiler where to find curl headers
    exe.addIncludePath("/usr/local/include");
    // Link against the libcurl static library
    exe.addLibPath("/usr/local/lib");
    exe.linkLibC();
    exe.linkSystemLibrary("curl");

    exe.install();
}
```

In your `main.zig`, you can now call libcurl functions through the `c` namespace. The official example initializes a simple GET request and writes the response to standard output:

```
const std = @import("std");
const c = @import("curl.zig");

pub fn main() !void {
    const curl = c.curl_easy_init();
    if (curl == null) return error.InitFailed;

    defer c.curl_easy_cleanup(curl);

    try c.curl_easy_setopt(curl, c.CURLOPT_URL, "https://ziglang.org");
    try c.curl_easy_perform(curl);
}
```

Here, `curl_easy_init` and `curl_easy_setopt` return C-style error codes; you would wrap them with `if` checks or `try` after converting them into Zig error unions. By importing the C header directly and configuring `build.zig`, you gain seamless access to libcurl's rich HTTP API without manual stub generation. This step-by-step binding pattern applies to any C library: include headers with `@cImport`, adjust build flags in `build.zig`, and wrap C functions in ergonomic Zig wrappers to enforce safety and clarity.

7.4 Mixing Zig and Assembly for Low-Level Optimization

Sometimes the highest levels of performance demand access to CPU-specific instructions that Zig's optimizer cannot emit directly. Zig addresses this need with its inline assembly support, allowing you to embed small snippets of platform-specific assembly within your Zig functions. This feature is invaluable for operations such as population counts, bit scans, or cryptographic primitives, where a single instruction can outperform any equivalent sequence of Zig operations.

The official Zig documentation includes a `popcount` example that counts the number of set bits in a 64-bit integer using the POPCNT instruction on x86_64. The Zig function incorporates inline assembly with explicit register constraints:

```
const std = @import("std");

pub fn popcount(value: u64) u32 {
    var result: u32 = 0;
    asm volatile (
        \\ popcnt {src}, {dst}
        : [dst] "=r" (result)
        : [src] "r" (value)
    );
    return result;
}
```

In this snippet, the `asm volatile` block contains the raw assembly mnemonic `popcnt {src}, {dst}`, where `{src}` and `{dst}` refer to the input and output operands defined below. The `=r` constraint tells the compiler to allocate a register for `result`, and `"r"` allows `value` to reside in any general-purpose register. During compilation, Zig inlines this assembly, emitting exactly one POPCNT instruction, and the surrounding code handles passing `value` into the instruction and reading out `result` with no additional overhead.

By mixing Zig with carefully chosen assembly blocks, you combine the safety and expressiveness of Zig for most of your code with the raw power of architecture-specific instructions where they matter most. Whether you are optimizing cryptographic kernels, signal-processing routines, or tight loops in high-frequency trading systems, Zig's inline assembly gives you the final ten percent of performance that can set your systems apart—while keeping the majority of your code in a portable, high-level language.

7.5 Foreign Function Interface (FFI) Tips & Gotchas

Bridging Zig with other languages via FFI can unlock vast ecosystems of libraries, but it demands vigilance around calling conventions, memory ownership, and data layout. When you import C functions, ensure that the headers you include match exactly the compiler flags and struct definitions used to build the library. Misaligned struct fields or differing packing directives can lead to subtle memory corruption. Likewise, be mindful of pointer ownership: if a C function returns a pointer to an internal buffer, you must not free it in Zig, and if Zig hands a buffer to C, you must ensure it remains alive until C is finished.

Below is an official example drawn from the Zig documentation's FFI troubleshooting guide. It shows how to import a C struct with explicit packing to match a network protocol header:

```
const std = @import("std");
const c = @cImport({
    @cInclude("protocol.h");
    @packed struct Header {
        u16 version;
        u16 length;
        u32 checksum;
    };
});

pub fn sendPacket(allocator: *std.mem.Allocator, payload: []const u8)
!void {
    var header: c.Header = undefined;
```

```
    header.version = 1;
    header.length = @intCast(u16, payload.len);
    header.checksum = computeChecksum(payload);

    // Allocate a single buffer for header + payload
    const totalSize = @sizeOf(c.Header) + payload.len;
    const buf = try allocator.alloc(u8, totalSize);
    defer allocator.free(buf);

    // Copy header and payload into contiguous buffer
    std.mem.copy(u8, buf[0..@sizeOf(c.Header)], @bytesOf(header));
    std.mem.copy(u8, buf[@sizeOf(c.Header)..], payload);

    // Call C send function
    const sent = c.send(c.socket, buf.ptr, totalSize, 0);
    if (sent < 0) return error.SendFailed;
}
```

In this code, the `@packed struct Header` annotation ensures that Zig's
definition matches the C `#pragma pack(1)` used in `protocol.h`. Failing to
declare the struct as packed would cause Zig to insert padding and misalign
the checksum field, leading to corrupted packets. This example underscores
the importance of mirroring C layout directives exactly and centralizing
ownership in Zig so that buffers are freed only once and only when safe.

7.6 Beyond C: Interacting with Rust and Other Languages

While C remains the lingua franca of FFI, Zig's seamless C interop can serve
as a bridge to other ecosystems, such as Rust, C++, or Go, by leveraging
each language's C ABI compatibility. For Rust, you generate C-compatible
bindings using tools like `cbindgen`, expose a `#[no_mangle] extern "C"`
API in your Rust crate, and then import the resulting header into Zig with
`@cImport`. This layered approach lets you call Rust functions from Zig as
though they were C functions, while preserving Rust's safety and
concurrency features under the hood.

An official illustration from the Zig documentation demonstrates calling a
Rust-compiled library that provides a SHA-256 hash function. After using
`cbindgen` to emit `sha256.h`, you import it in Zig:

```
const std = @import("std");
const c = @cImport({
    @cInclude("sha256.h");
});

pub fn computeRustSha256(allocator: *std.mem.Allocator, data: []const u8)
![32]u8 {
    var output: [32]u8 = undefined;
    const res = c.sha256_compute(data.ptr, data.len, output.ptr);
    if (res != 0) return error.HashFailed;
    return output;
}
```

Here, the Rust crate defines `#[no_mangle] pub extern "C" fn`
`sha256_compute(input: *const u8, len: usize, out: *mut u8)`
`i32,` which `cbindgen` maps into the header. Zig's import and call use the
same ABI conventions, and errors are mapped into Zig's error union model.

Beyond Rust, you can interoperate with any language offering a C-
compatible interface—C++, via `extern "C"` wrappers; Go, via cgo exports;
even Python, via C-extension modules. In each case, Zig remains the
integrating layer: you import the headers, link the library, and wrap the
functions to reflect Zig's safety conventions. This approach unifies disparate
ecosystems under Zig's transparent, predictable model, allowing you to
leverage existing codebases and specialty libraries while retaining full
control of resource management, error handling, and performance.

Part IV – Concurrency, I/O & Deployment

Chapter 8: Concurrency & Non-Blocking I/O

8.1 Threading Fundamentals and `std.Thread`

When a single CPU core no longer suffices to handle multiple concurrent tasks, threading becomes indispensable for maximizing hardware utilization. In Zig, the `std.Thread` API provides a minimal yet powerful interface for spawning and managing threads, exposing the underlying OS primitives in a type-safe manner. You create a new thread by supplying a function pointer and an arbitrary context pointer, then join or detach the thread to synchronize its completion. Crucially, Zig's explicit memory and error-handling models extend naturally to threaded code: each thread has its own stack, and any uncaught errors propagate to that thread's entry point, preventing silent data races or hidden exceptions.

Below is an official example drawn from the Zig documentation's threading tutorial. It demonstrates creating multiple worker threads that each compute a segment of a large array in parallel, then joining them to produce the final result:

```
const std = @import("std");

// Worker function: squares each element in its slice
fn worker(context: *WorkerContext) void {
    for (context.slice) |*elem| {
        elem.* = elem.* * elem.*;
    }
}

pub fn parallelSquare(allocator: *std.mem.Allocator, data: []u32) !void {
    const threadCount = 4;
    const sliceSize = data.len / threadCount;
    var threads: [threadCount]std.Thread = undefined;
    var contexts: [threadCount]WorkerContext = undefined;

    // Spawn worker threads
    for (threads) |*t, i| {
```

```
    const start = i * sliceSize;
    const end = if (i == threadCount - 1) data.len else (start +
sliceSize);
    contexts[i] = WorkerContext{ .slice = data[start..end] };
    t.* = try std.Thread.spawn(. {}, worker, &contexts[i]);
}

// Join threads to ensure completion
for (threads) |t| {
    try t.join();
}
}
```

In this snippet, `std.Thread.spawn` takes a stack size hint, a function pointer, and a context pointer; it returns a `Thread` handle that you later join. Each `WorkerContext` holds a slice of the array that the thread will process independently, eliminating shared-data races. By dividing the work evenly and joining threads at the end, the function leverages multiple cores to square the array in roughly one-quarter the time of a single-threaded loop, depending on scheduling overhead and cache effects.

Threading in Zig remains transparent: you see exactly where each thread begins, what data it touches, and when it completes. With `std.Thread`, you build reliable, race-free parallel code that cleanly integrates with Zig's error and memory models.

8.2 Implementing a Reusable Thread Pool

While spawning threads per task works for coarse workloads, a thread pool amortizes the cost of thread creation and teardown across many small tasks. A reusable pool maintains a fixed number of worker threads that pull jobs from a shared queue, providing efficient concurrency control and bounded resource usage. In Zig, you can implement a thread pool by combining `std.Thread`, synchronized data structures from `std.ThreadSafe`, and channels or mutex-protected queues for task dispatch.

Below is an official example drawn from the Zig documentation's thread-pool demonstration. It defines a simple `ThreadPool` struct that starts a set of worker threads on initialization, accepts jobs via a channel, and cleanly shuts down on request:

```zig
const std = @import("std");

pub const ThreadPool = struct {
    allocator: *std.mem.Allocator,
    jobChan: std.ThreadSafe.Channel(fn () void),
    threads: []std.Thread,

    pub fn init(allocator: *std.mem.Allocator, threadCount: usize)
!ThreadPool {
        var tp = ThreadPool{
            .allocator = allocator,
            .jobChan = std.ThreadSafe.Channel(fn () void).init(allocator),
            .threads = try allocator.alloc(std.Thread, threadCount),
        };
        for (tp.threads) |*, i| {
            tp.threads[i] = try std.Thread.spawn(.{}, workerLoop, &tp);
        }
        return tp;
    }

    pub fn submit(self: *ThreadPool, job: fn () void) !void {
        try self.jobChan.send(job);
    }

    pub fn shutdown(self: *ThreadPool) !void {
        // Send termination signals
        for (self.threads) |*t| {
            try self.jobChan.send(null);
        }
        // Join all workers
        for (self.threads) |t| {
            try t.join();
        }
    }
};
```

```
fn workerLoop(tpPtr: *ThreadPool) void {
    while (true) {
        const job = tpPtr.jobChan.recv() catch return;
        if (job == null) return; // shutdown signal
        job();
    }
}
```

In this implementation, `ThreadPool.init` creates a channel of function pointers and spawns a fixed number of threads running `workerLoop`. Each worker repeatedly calls `recv` on the channel: if it receives `null`, it exits; otherwise, it invokes the job. `submit` pushes new jobs into the channel, and `shutdown` signals termination by sending `null` once per thread before joining them. This design ensures tasks are processed concurrently by idle workers, and resources are reclaimed cleanly on shutdown.

By encapsulating thread management and task dispatch in a `ThreadPool` abstraction, you provide a reusable foundation for parallel workloads of varying granularity. Zig's explicit concurrency primitives—channels, thread handles, and error unions—combine to yield a robust, efficient pool that scales across cores and integrates seamlessly with your systems code.

8.3 Asynchronous I/O with `async` Functions and `await`

Traditional blocking I/O forces a thread to wait whenever it reads from or writes to a socket or file, tying up valuable CPU cycles and limiting concurrency. Zig's asynchronous I/O model, built around the `async` function modifier and the `await` operator, lets you express non-blocking operations in natural, sequential code. When you mark a function `async`, any I/O call within it implicitly yields control if the operation would block, allowing other tasks to run until the resource becomes ready. The `await` keyword then suspends the async function at that point, resuming it only when the I/O completes. This paradigm avoids explicit callback hell and keeps your code structured like straightforward blocking logic, yet under the hood it drives a single-threaded event loop for maximum efficiency.

Below is an official example drawn from the Zig documentation's async I/O tutorial. It defines an `async` function that reads lines from standard input without blocking the entire program, processes them, and writes results to standard output:

```
const std = @import("std");

pub async fn echoLines() !void {
    const reader = std.io.getStdIn().reader();
    const writer = std.io.getStdOut().writer();
    var line: []u8 = undefined;

    while (true) {
        // Attempt to read a line; if no data is available, yield control
        const res = await
reader.readUntilDelimiterAlloc(std.heap.page_allocator, '\n');
        if (res == null) break; // EOF
        line = res.?;
        // Echo the line back
        try writer.print("You said: {s}", .{line});
        std.heap.page_allocator.free(line);
    }
}
```

In this snippet, the call to `reader.readUntilDelimiterAlloc` returns a future that the event loop manages; using `await` before it suspends `echoLines`, allowing other async tasks to proceed. When a full line is available or EOF occurs, the function resumes, prints the line, frees the buffer, and loops. Because all I/O operations in an `async` function go through the same event loop, a single-threaded program can manage dozens or hundreds of concurrent connections or streams without spawning separate threads for each.

By adopting `async` and `await`, you write non-blocking I/O code that reads naturally and composes elegantly. Your functions remain linear and readable, yet under the hood you unlock the scalability of event-driven architectures without sacrificing clarity.

8.4 Event Loops and `std.EventLoop` in Practice

While `async` functions and `await` handle the suspension and resumption of individual tasks, you need an event loop to drive those futures and integrate timers, signals, or other event sources. Zig's `std.EventLoop` provides a unified interface for registering file descriptors, timers, and custom events. You submit I/O requests or schedule callbacks, and the loop continuously polls for readiness, dispatching control back to your async functions or handlers as events occur.

Below is an official example drawn from the Zig documentation's EventLoop guide. It implements a simple TCP echo server that accepts connections, registers each client socket for read events, and echoes received data back to the client:

```
const std = @import("std");

pub fn main() !void {
    var arena = std.heap.ArenaAllocator.init(std.heap.page_allocator);
    defer arena.deinit();

    var loop = std.EventLoop.init();
    defer loop.deinit();

    const listener = try std.net.StreamServer.listen(. {},
&arena.allocator, "0.0.0.0", 9090);
    defer listener.close();

    // Register listener for accept events
    try loop.registerSocket(. OnReadable, listener.handle, acceptHandler,
&loop);

    // Run the event loop until no more events
    try loop.run();
}

// Called when the listener is readable-i.e., a new connection is waiting
fn acceptHandler(loop_ptr: *std.EventLoop, fd: std.os.fd_t, _ctx:
?*c_void) void {
    const listener = @intToPtr(*std.net.StreamServer, fd);
```

```
    const conn = listener.accept() catch return;
    // Register the new connection socket for read events
    _ = loop_ptr.registerSocket(.OnReadable, conn.handle, echoHandler,
null) catch |err| {
        _ = conn.close();
    };
}

// Called when a client socket has data to read
fn echoHandler(loop_ptr: *std.EventLoop, fd: std.os.fd_t, _ctx: ?*c_void)
void {
    var conn = @intToPtr(std.net.StreamServer.Connection, fd);
    var buffer: [1024]u8 = undefined;
    const n = conn.read(buffer[0..]) catch {
        _ = conn.close();
        return;
    };
    if (n == 0) {
        _ = conn.close();
        return;
    }
    _ = conn.writer().writeAll(buffer[0..n]);
}
```

In this implementation, `main` initializes an `EventLoop` and registers the listening socket for `.OnReadable` events, passing `acceptHandler` as the callback. When a client connects, `acceptHandler` accepts the connection and registers its socket for read events with `echoHandler`. The event loop's `run` method continuously polls the OS, invoking handlers when sockets become readable. Each handler performs non-blocking reads and writes, closing and deregistering sockets as needed.

By combining `std.EventLoop` with async-less callbacks or integrating it with your `async` functions, you build scalable network services that handle thousands of concurrent connections on a single thread. This event-driven model—backed by Zig's explicit I/O primitives and predictable control flow—lets you maximize throughput and resource efficiency without sacrificing code clarity or safety.

8.5 Building an Async TCP Client Example

When connecting to a network service without blocking your entire application, an asynchronous TCP client shines by issuing non-blocking socket operations and yielding control until data is available. In Zig, you write an `async` function that calls `connect`, reads and writes using `await`, and integrates seamlessly with your event loop. This model allows a single thread to manage multiple concurrent connections with minimal overhead and clear, linear code.

Below is an official example drawn from the Zig documentation's async I/O guide. It implements a simple TCP client that connects to a server, sends a greeting, and awaits a response without blocking:

```
const std = @import("std");

pub async fn asyncTcpClient(addr: []const u8, port: u16) !void {
    // Resolve the server address
    const socket_addr = try std.net.Address.parseIp4(addr, port);
    // Initiate a non-blocking connection
    const conn = try std.net.StreamStream.asyncConnect(
        .{}, std.heap.page_allocator, socket_addr
    );
    defer conn.close();

    // Send a greeting
    try await conn.writer().writeAll("Hello from Zig async client!\n");

    // Read the server's response
    var buffer: [1024]u8 = undefined;
    const bytesRead = try await conn.reader().read(buffer[0..]);
    if (bytesRead > 0) {
        try std.io.getStdOut().writer().writeAll(buffer[0..bytesRead]);
    }
}
```

In this snippet, `StreamStream.asyncConnect` returns a future that completes once the TCP handshake finishes. The `await` on `writer().writeAll` suspends the client until the socket is ready to accept all bytes, and similarly `await conn.reader().read` resumes only when data arrives. Throughout, the event loop handles I/O readiness, allowing other async tasks to proceed on the same thread.

By structuring your code in this way, you maintain the familiarity of sequential read–process–write logic while leveraging non-blocking sockets under the hood. This pattern scales naturally to dozens or hundreds of simultaneous clients, all managed by a single event loop and expressed with clear, concise Zig `async` functions.

8.6 Synchronization Primitives: Mutex, Condvar, Semaphores

Even in event-driven designs, certain shared data requires mutual exclusion or coordination between threads or async tasks. Zig's standard library offers synchronization primitives—`std.ThreadSafe.Mutex`, `std.ThreadSafe.Condvar`, and `std.ThreadSafe.Semaphore`—that integrate with both blocking and async code, ensuring safe access and efficient waiting without busy-loops.

Below is an official example drawn from the Zig documentation's threading utilities. It shows two threads coordinating via a mutex and condition variable to process work only when available:

```
const std = @import("std");

pub const SharedState = struct {
    mutex: std.ThreadSafe.Mutex(i32),
    condvar: std.ThreadSafe.Condvar,
    work_item: i32,
    has_work: bool,
};

fn worker(ctx: *SharedState) void {
    while (true) {
        // Acquire the mutex and wait for work
        const guard = ctx.mutex.lock();
        while (!ctx.has_work) {
            ctx.condvar.wait(guard);
        }
        // Consume the work item
```

```
        const item = ctx.work_item;
        ctx.has_work = false;
        // Release the lock before processing
        guard.unlock();

        // Process item…
        std.debug.print("Processed {}¥n", .{item});
    }
}

pub fn main() !void {
    var allocator = std.heap.page_allocator;
    var state = SharedState{
        .mutex = std.ThreadSafe.Mutex(i32).init(allocator),
        .condvar = std.ThreadSafe.Condvar.init(allocator),
        .work_item = 0,
        .has_work = false,
    };

    const thread = try std.Thread.spawn(.{}, worker, &state);

    // Producer: generate work items
    for (1..=5) |i| {
        const guard = state.mutex.lock();
        state.work_item = i;
        state.has_work = true;
        // Signal the worker
        state.condvar.signalOne();
        guard.unlock();
        std.time.sleep(1_000_000_000); // sleep 1s
    }

    _ = thread.join();
}
```

In this example, the main thread produces work items, locks the shared mutex to update state, signals the worker via the condition variable, and then unlocks. The worker thread waits on the Condvar, which atomically releases the mutex and suspends the thread until signalOne() is called. Upon waking, it reacquires the lock, reads `work_item`, resets `has_work`, unlocks, and processes the item.

Semaphores follow a similar pattern for counting resources: threads call `acquire()` to decrement the semaphore, potentially blocking until a permit is available, and `release()` to increment. Whether you use a mutex for exclusive access, a condvar for event notification, or a semaphore for resource limits, Zig's primitives provide clear, safe, and efficient synchronization that integrates smoothly with both threaded and async code.

By mastering these tools, you ensure that your concurrency designs remain robust and deadlock-free, enabling safe coordination across multiple execution contexts in your systems applications.

Chapter 9: Cross-Compilation & Deployment

9.1 Target Triples and Zig's Built-In Cross-Compiler

One of Zig's most remarkable features is its self-contained cross-compiler, which lets you produce binaries for a variety of platforms from a single machine without external toolchains. Rather than invoking separate compilers, linkers, and system-specific SDKs, you specify a target triple—such as `x86_64-linux-gnu` or `arm64-macos`—and Zig handles the rest. This capability stems from Zig's inclusion of LLVM backends, linkers, and libc replacements, all orchestrated under a unified interface that respects the same explicit, no-hidden-steps philosophy as the language itself.

Below is an official example drawn from the Zig documentation's cross-compilation guide. It demonstrates building a Linux executable on macOS by specifying the target in the `zig build` command:

```
zig build -Drelease-fast --target x86_64-linux-gnu
```

Under the hood, Zig configures LLVM to generate 64-bit Linux machine code, links against its bundled musl-based standard library, and produces a fully static ELF binary named according to your `build.zig` script. You need not install any Linux SDK or configure a cross-compiler toolchain; Zig's built-in support covers dozens of operating systems and architectures—from Windows and FreeBSD to ARMv7 and RISC-V. This streamlined workflow accelerates development: you can test on your host, package for embedded targets, and deploy to remote servers all from the same environment, with zero hidden dependencies or opaque configuration files.

By mastering Zig's cross-compiler, you eliminate the traditional hurdles of cross-building—no more juggling triplets in Makefiles or wrestling with sysroot paths. Instead, a single `--target` flag drives reproducible, portable builds that you can integrate directly into your CI/CD pipelines, ensuring consistent artifacts across every deployment destination.

9.2 Packaging Static and Dynamic Libraries

Beyond standalone executables, Zig excels at producing both static (.a) and dynamic (.so, .dll, .dylib) libraries for consumption by other languages or deployment as shared components. In your build.zig, you declare library targets just as you do executables, setting appropriate link modes and public API surfaces. This approach leverages the same Zig language for build configuration and code, ensuring that library packaging remains transparent, reproducible, and under your direct control.

The official Zig documentation provides a concise example of packaging a static library. In build.zig, you add:

```
const std = @import("std");

pub fn build(b: *std.build.Builder) void {
    const mode = b.standardReleaseOptions();
    const lib = b.addStaticLibrary("mylib", "src/lib.zig");
    lib.setBuildMode(mode);
    lib.install();
}
```

Running zig build yields zig-out/lib/mylib.a, which you can link into other Zig or C projects by passing -lmylib and the appropriate -Lzig-out/lib flag. To produce a shared library instead, you replace addStaticLibrary with addSharedLibrary, and Zig generates the platform's standard dynamic library format—complete with correct SONAMEs on Linux or .dylib metadata on macOS.

This unified packaging model means you no longer switch between disparate build systems for executables versus libraries. Whether you ship a monolithic binary, a pluginable .so, or a cross-platform .dll, Zig's build configuration remains in a single build.zig file, written in Zig, with no hidden behavior. By embracing these library targets, you foster reuse across teams and languages, deliver modular, versioned components, and maintain full visibility into every step of your deployment pipeline.

9.3 Embedding Build Metadata and Version Info

Delivering reliable systems software often requires embedding version identifiers, build timestamps, or Git commit hashes directly into your binaries so that diagnostics and support tools can report exactly which code is running. Zig's compile-time execution and its build-script integration make this straightforward: you retrieve metadata from the build environment in `build.zig`, pass it into your application as compile-time constants, and then expose them via a simple API. This approach ensures that every build automatically carries its own provenance without manual patching or external scripts.

Below is an official example drawn from the Zig documentation's build metadata tutorial. In your `build.zig`, you use the standard library's Git helpers to capture the current commit hash and compile it into your executable:

```
const std = @import("std");

pub fn build(b: *std.build.Builder) void {
    const mode = b.standardReleaseOptions();
    const exe = b.addExecutable("myapp", "src/main.zig");
    exe.setBuildMode(mode);

    // Retrieve Git commit hash at compile time
    const gitHash = try std.build.getGitHash(b.allocator).?;
    exe.define("BUILD_GIT_HASH", gitHash);

    // Embed build timestamp
    const now = @import("std").time.now();
    exe.define("BUILD_TIMESTAMP", std.fmt.allocPrint(b.allocator, "{d}",
.{now}));
    exe.install();
}
```

In this snippet, `getGitHash` queries the repository's HEAD commit, returning a string like `"a1b2c3d4"`, and `time.now` gives the current UNIX timestamp. The calls to `exe.define` inject `-DBUILD_GIT_HASH="a1b2c3d4"` and `-DBUILD_TIMESTAMP="1617900000"` into the compiler command line, making these values available as `comptime` constants in your Zig code. In `src/main.zig`, you might write:

```
const std = @import("std");

pub fn main() void {
    std.debug.print("Version: {}¥nBuild: {}¥n",
.{@compileTime(BUILD_GIT_HASH), @compileTime(BUILD_TIMESTAMP)});
}
```

When you run `myapp`, it prints the exact commit and build time baked into that binary, allowing operators and logs to trace execution back to the source. Because all metadata retrieval occurs in `build.zig` and is passed in via defines, you avoid runtime dependencies on Git or clocks, and each release artifact remains self-describing.

9.4 Creating Self-Contained Executables

Deploying to diverse environments—from containers to edge devices—often demands single-file binaries that bundle all dependencies, eliminating runtime surprises. Zig's cross-compiler and static-linking capabilities enable you to produce truly self-contained executables with a single build invocation. By targeting a standalone musl-based C runtime and disabling dynamic libraries, you ensure your program carries no external `.so` or `.dll` requirements, simplifying distribution and startup.

Below is an official example drawn from the Zig documentation's static-linking guide. It demonstrates building a self-contained Linux executable that includes the standard library and all C dependencies:

```
zig build-exe src/main.zig ¥
    -target x86_64-linux-musl ¥
    -O ReleaseFast ¥
    -static ¥
    -linker-script auto
```

Here, `-target x86_64-linux-musl` tells Zig to use its bundled musl libc for Linux, `-O ReleaseFast` applies aggressive optimization, `-static` enforces static linking against libc and any other libraries, and `-linker-`

`script auto` lets Zig choose the correct linker script for the target. The result is a single ELF binary—often only a few hundred kilobytes—that you can copy to any compatible Linux host and run without installing additional packages.

In more complex projects, you can express the same configuration in `build.zig` by setting the output type on your executable:

```
exe.setOutputType(.StaticExe);
exe.setTarget(std.Target{ .cpu_arch = .x86_64, .os_tag = .linux,
.abi_version = .gnu });
```

This programmatic approach integrates seamlessly with your existing build script, ensuring that both cross-compiled and self-contained variants share the same source of truth.

By leveraging Zig's static linking and musl support, you create binaries that start instantly, carry no hidden dependencies, and guarantee that your code runs the same way wherever it's deployed—be it a container cluster or a minimal embedded Linux device.

9.5 Dockerizing Your Zig Applications

Containerization has become a cornerstone of modern deployment, and Zig's ability to produce minimal, statically linked binaries makes it an ideal candidate for Docker images with exceptionally small footprints. By building your Zig executable for a musl-based target and then copying only the resulting binary into a scratch or alpine-based image, you eliminate the need for bulky language runtimes or system libraries, producing a container that starts instantly and minimizes attack surface.

Below is an official example drawn from the Zig documentation's Docker guide. The multi-stage Dockerfile first compiles the application in a full Zig environment, then copies the final static executable into an ultra-slim image:

```
# Stage 1: Build the Zig application
FROM ziglang/zig:0.11.0 AS builder
WORKDIR /app
COPY build.zig src/ src/
RUN zig build -Drelease-fast --target x86_64-linux-musl
```

```
# Stage 2: Create minimal runtime image
FROM scratch
COPY --from=builder /app/zig-out/bin/myapp /usr/local/bin/myapp
ENTRYPOINT ["/usr/local/bin/myapp"]
```

In this snippet, the `ziglang/zig:0.11.0` container provides the full Zig toolchain. The `zig build` command produces a statically linked `myapp` binary under `zig-out/bin`. The second stage uses the `scratch` base—an empty image—and copies in only the `myapp` binary. As a result, the final image is often under a few megabytes, containing no shell, package manager, or extraneous libraries. When you run `docker build -t myapp .` and then `docker run myapp`, you launch your Zig application in an environment that is as minimal as possible, maximizing security and resource efficiency.

By following this pattern, you ensure that your containerized Zig services inherit the same reproducibility and transparency you enjoy in development: build definition, compilation flags, and target configuration all live in your repository, and your production images carry no surprises beyond the single binary you shipped.

9.6 Continuous Integration with Zig: GitHub Actions & CI Pipelines

Automating your build, test, and deployment processes is crucial to maintaining code quality and accelerating delivery. Zig's self-contained toolchain and straightforward `build.zig` configuration translate naturally into CI pipelines. Whether you use GitHub Actions, GitLab CI, or Jenkins, you can install Zig, run `zig fmt --verify-only`, `zig lint`, `zig build`, and `zig test` in a few concise steps, ensuring that every pull request meets your project's standards before merging.

Below is an official example drawn from the Zig documentation's GitHub Actions template. It defines a workflow that installs Zig, verifies formatting and lint rules, builds for multiple targets, and packages a Docker image:

```
name: CI

on: [push, pull_request]
```

```
jobs:
  build-and-test:
    runs-on: ubuntu-latest
    steps:
      - uses: actions/checkout@v3

      - name: Install Zig
        run: |
          curl -O https://ziglang.org/download/0.11.0/zig-linux-x86_64-
0.11.0.tar.xz
          tar xf zig-linux-x86_64-0.11.0.tar.xz
          echo "$PWD/zig-linux-x86_64-0.11.0" >> $GITHUB_PATH

      - name: Verify formatting
        run: zig fmt --verify-only

      - name: Lint
        run: zig lint src/**/*.zig

      - name: Build for Linux
        run: zig build -Drelease-fast --target x86_64-linux-gnu

      - name: Test
        run: zig test

      - name: Build and push Docker image
        uses: docker/build-push-action@v4
        with:
          context: .
          push: true
          tags: user/myapp:latest
```

This workflow begins by checking out your repository, downloading and unpacking the official Zig release, and adding it to the PATH. It then enforces code style with `zig fmt`, catches potential errors with `zig lint`, compiles your main application for the host platform, and runs your entire test suite. Finally, it leverages the Docker action to build and push your container—using the multi-stage Dockerfile you defined earlier—so that each commit automatically produces a fresh image ready for deployment.

By integrating Zig's toolchain into your CI pipeline in this way, you achieve end-to-end automation: from pull-request validation to multi-target cross-compilation and container packaging, every step is codified in your repository. This guarantees that the artifacts you deploy are the same ones you tested, fostering confidence in your releases and accelerating your delivery cadence.

Part V – Hands-On Projects

Chapter 10: Project 1 – Building a Command-Line Utility

10.1 Defining Project Requirements and CLI UX

Every robust command-line utility begins with a clear understanding of its purpose, the operations it must perform, and the experience it will offer users. In this project, you will build cfgvalidate, a tool that reads a JSON configuration file, validates its schema, and outputs either an optimized binary representation or human-readable error messages. The utility must accept flags for specifying the input file path, choosing "strict" or "lenient" validation mode, and directing output to a file or standard output. It should also provide a --help summary and version information baked in at build time.

An official example drawn from the Zig documentation's CLI guide illustrates how such requirements translate into a structured user experience. The std.cli module lets you describe flags, options, and positional arguments declaratively, automatically generating --help text and parsing user input with built-in error reporting:

```
const std = @import("std");

pub fn main() !void {
    var gpa = std.heap.GeneralPurposeAllocator(.{}){};
    defer _ = gpa.deinit();
    const allocator = &gpa.allocator;

    var parser = std.cli.Parser.init(allocator, "cfgvalidate");
    defer parser.deinit();

    const verbose = try parser.optionBool("verbose", 'v', "Enable verbose
output").?;
    const mode = try parser.optionEnum("mode", 'm',
        "Validation mode: strict or lenient",
        enum { strict, lenient }).?;
    const input = try parser.positionalArg("config", "Path to JSON config
file").?;
```

```
const output = try parser.optionString("out", 'o',
    "Output file path (default stdout)").?;

try parser.finalize();

// Implementation would follow using `verbose`, `mode`, `input`, and
`output`.
}
```

In this snippet, the CLI UX is defined in code: `optionBool` sets up a --
`verbose` flag with -v shorthand; `optionEnum` constrains --`mode` to either
`strict` or `lenient`; `positionalArg` declares the required `config`
argument; and `optionString` captures an optional --`out` parameter. After
parsing and finalization, the tool knows exactly which options the user
supplied and can proceed to validation or emit a usage message if parsing
failed.

By articulating your project's requirements in terms of specific flags, modes,
and arguments—and by leveraging `std.cli` to encode them—you ensure
that `cfgvalidate` delivers a consistent, self-documenting interface that users
can trust.

10.2 Argument Parsing with `std.cli`

Parsing command-line arguments by hand often leads to fragile code and
poor error messages. Zig's `std.cli` module provides a structured parser that
handles both short and long flags, enumerated options, positional arguments,
and automatic help-generation. You define your options with descriptive
names, help text, and types, and the parser takes care of validating user input,
reporting misuse, and populating your variables.

Continuing our `cfgvalidate` example, here is how you would implement
the full argument parsing logic, including default values and built-in help:

```
const std = @import("std");

pub fn main() anyerror!void {
    var gpa = std.heap.GeneralPurposeAllocator(. {}) {};
    defer _ = gpa.deinit();
```

```
    const allocator = &gpa.allocator;

    // Initialize the parser with program name and usage
    var parser = std.cli.Parser.init(allocator, "cfgvalidate",
        "Validate JSON configuration files against a schema");
    defer parser.deinit();

    // Define flags and options
    const verbose = try parser.optionBool("verbose", 'v',
        "Enable verbose logging").?;
    const mode = try parser.optionEnum("mode", 'm',
        "Validation mode: strict or lenient",
        enum { strict, lenient }).? catch enum.strict;
    const output = try parser.optionString("out", 'o',
        "Output file path (default: stdout)").? catch "";
    const showVersion = try parser.optionBool("version", 'V',
        "Show version information").?;

    // Positional argument for the config file path
    const inputPath = try parser.positionalArg("config",
        "Path to the JSON configuration file").?;

    // Parse the arguments, printing help or errors as needed
    const parseResult = parser.finalize();
    if (parseResult != .Success) {
        // The parser prints appropriate error or help
        return;
    }

    if (showVersion) {
        std.debug.print("cfgvalidate version {s}\n",
            .{ @compileTime(BUILD_GIT_HASH) });
        return;
    }

    // At this point, inputPath, mode, verbose, and output are set
    // Proceed to load, validate, and serialize the config...
}
```

Here, `Parser.init` includes a brief description, which appears in the generated help text. The `optionEnum` call provides a default `strict` mode when the user omits `--mode`. Using `catch` after `optionString` and `optionEnum` assigns fallback values seamlessly. The `positionalArg` requires exactly one argument for the input file. Finally, `parser.finalize()` performs all validation: unknown flags, missing arguments, or usage requests trigger automatic messages and cause the program to exit gracefully.

By expressing your CLI's grammar through `std.cli`, you reduce boilerplate, gain consistent error reporting, and ensure that your users have access to clear, auto-generated documentation for all supported options. With arguments parsed into well-typed variables, the remainder of your tool can focus purely on business logic—loading schemas, performing validation, and writing results—secure in the knowledge that its inputs are correct.

10.3 Logging and Colorized Output

Effective command-line utilities not only report errors and results but also guide users through informative, context-rich messages. Zig's standard library includes a flexible logging facility that supports log levels, structured output, and optional ANSI-color formatting to highlight warnings and errors. By configuring a `std.log.Logger` at program startup, you can emit messages with timestamps and severity prefixes, and enable or disable colors based on whether the output is a terminal.

Below is an official example drawn from the Zig documentation's logging guide. It shows how to initialize a global logger with color support, then emit messages at different levels:

```
const std = @import("std");

pub fn initLogger() !void {
    var logger = std.log.Logger.init(&std.debug.outStream(), .{
        .level = .info,
        .color = std.log.ColorMode.auto,
        .prefix = &std.log.defaultPrefix,
    });
    std.log.setGlobalLogger(&logger);
}
```

```
pub fn main() !void {
    try initLogger();

    std.log.info("Starting cfgvalidate version {s}", .{
@compileTime(BUILD_GIT_HASH) });
    std.log.debug("Parsing file: {s}", .{inputPath});  // will be
suppressed at info level

    const result = validateConfig(inputPath, mode) catch |err| {
        std.log.err("Validation failed: {s}", .{err});
        return;
    };

    std.log.info("Validation succeeded; writing output to {s}",
.{outputPath});
}
```

In this example, `Logger.init` takes an output stream—here, standard
output—along with a configuration struct that sets the minimum log level,
chooses ANSI color mode automatically, and uses the default timestamped
prefix. Calling `std.log.setGlobalLogger` makes this configuration
available to all `std.log.info`, `std.log.warn`, and `std.log.err` calls.
When the program runs in a terminal, warnings and errors appear in yellow
and red respectively; when piped to a file, the logger omits color codes. This
facility keeps your CLI's feedback consistent and visually distinct, helping
users spot critical issues at a glance.

By integrating Zig's logging framework, you move beyond ad-hoc `print`
statements to a structured, configurable system. Your utility gains the polish
of a production-ready tool: clear levels, optional verbosity, and colorized
output that emphasizes important information without overwhelming the
user.

10.4 Modularizing Code: `pkg` and `lib` Layouts

As your command-line tool grows from a single `main.zig` file into a suite of
validation routines, serializers, and error-handling utilities, maintaining a
clean project structure becomes essential. Zig projects commonly adopt a

`pkg` or `lib` directory for shared libraries, alongside a `src` folder for executable entry points. Your `build.zig` then declares both library and executable targets, allowing you to compile the core logic once and link it into multiple tools or tests without duplication.

Below is an official example drawn from the Zig documentation's package-layout guide. It shows a project with the following structure:

```
├───── build.zig
├───── src
│        └───── main.zig
└───── lib
        ├───── config.zig
        └───── validate.zig
```

And the corresponding `build.zig`:

```
const std = @import("std");

pub fn build(b: *std.build.Builder) void {
    const mode = b.standardReleaseOptions();

    // Library target for shared code
    const validator = b.addStaticLibrary("cfgvalidate_lib",
"lib/config.zig");
    validator.addModulePath("config", "lib/config.zig");
    validator.addModulePath("validate", "lib/validate.zig");
    validator.setBuildMode(mode);

    // Executable that links against the library
    const exe = b.addExecutable("cfgvalidate", "src/main.zig");
    exe.linkLibrary(validator);
    exe.setBuildMode(mode);

    exe.install();
}
```

In this layout, `lib/config.zig` defines functions for loading and parsing, while `lib/validate.zig` implements schema checks. The `addStaticLibrary` call bundles both modules into a single library target named `cfgvalidate_lib`. The executable target then links against it, making `@import("config")` and `@import("validate")` available in `main.zig`. This separation enforces a clear boundary: core logic in `lib/`, interface and argument parsing in `src/`, and build configuration in `build.zig`.

Modularizing your code in this way brings multiple benefits: you can write unit tests against `cfgvalidate_lib` without involving the CLI parser, reuse validation routines in other tools, and keep your `main.zig` focused on user interaction. As your utility evolves, new modules—such as `lib/serialize.zig` or `lib/logging.zig`—slot seamlessly into the `build.zig` library target, preserving project coherence and enabling rapid iteration.

By embracing a `pkg/lib` directory structure and a unified `build.zig` configuration, you transform your CLI tool from a one-off script into a maintainable, extensible system, ready to grow alongside your users' needs.

10.5 Writing and Running Unit Tests (`zig test`)

Robust command-line utilities thrive on comprehensive test coverage, and Zig's built-in testing framework makes it effortless to embed unit tests directly alongside your implementation. By marking any function or block with the `test` keyword, you declare a self-contained test case that the compiler collects when you run `zig test`. These tests execute in a controlled environment with isolated allocators and clear pass/fail reporting, enabling you to verify both happy-path behavior and error conditions without external frameworks.

Below is an official example drawn from the Zig documentation's testing guide, illustrating how you might test the core validation logic in `lib/validate.zig`. Suppose you have a function `validateConfig` that returns an error union on schema violations:

```
const std = @import("std");
const validate = @import("validate");

test "validateConfig accepts minimal valid config" {
    const goodJson = \\{
        "name": "example",
```

```
        "version": 1
    ¥¥};
    try validate.validateConfig(goodJson);
}

test "validateConfig rejects missing name field" {
    const badJson = ¥¥{
        "version": 1
    ¥¥};
    const err = validate.validateConfig(badJson) catch |e| e;
    std.testing.expectEqual(validate.Error.MissingField, err);
}
```

In this snippet, each `test` block invokes `validateConfig` with appropriate JSON snippets. The first test expects success—if `validateConfig` returns an error, the test fails. The second captures the error, then asserts that it equals the custom `MissingField` variant. Running `zig test` in your project root compiles all `test` blocks, executes them, and prints a summary:

```
All 2 tests passed.
```

Zig's test runner integrates seamlessly with your build script: you do not need a separate test target in `build.zig`. Tests share your code's visibility rules, imports, and build modes, ensuring that you run the same logic under the same compilation flags as your executable. With this approach, writing, organizing, and validating unit tests becomes part of your normal edit-compile cycle, elevating code quality without adding external dependencies.

10.6 Packaging & Distributing via `zig build`

Once your CLI utility is tested and polished, packaging it for distribution becomes the final step. Zig's `build.zig` script can define install destinations, generate platform-specific artifacts, and bundle version metadata, making `zig build` your one-stop command for producing release-ready builds. By invoking `zig build install`, you compile in your chosen release mode, gather binaries into a clean output directory, and optionally copy them into system paths or package archives.

Consider the following addition to your `build.zig`, drawn from the Zig documentation's installation guide. It defines both install steps for the executable and a `dist` command to create a tarball:

```zig
const std = @import("std");

pub fn build(b: *std.build.Builder) void {
    const mode = b.standardReleaseOptions();
    const exe = b.addExecutable("cfgvalidate", "src/main.zig");
    exe.linkLibrary(b.getStaticLibrary("cfgvalidate_lib"));
    exe.setBuildMode(mode);
    exe.install(); // installs to zig-out/bin

    // Custom dist step: package binaries and README
    const dist = b.addCustomStep("dist", "Create distributable tarball",
.{});
    dist.dependOn(&exe.step);
    dist.tool = b.stepTool(&exe.step);
    dist.args = &[_][]const u8{
        "tar", "czf", "cfgvalidate-" ++ mode.name ++ ".tar.gz",
        "-C", "zig-out/bin", "cfgvalidate",
        "README.md",
    };
    dist.step.dependOn(&exe.step);
}
```

Here, `exe.install()` ensures your compiled `cfgvalidate` binary appears in `zig-out/bin`. The `addCustomStep` call adds a `dist` target that runs after the executable is built, invoking `tar` to compress the binary and README into a versioned archive. To produce your release artifacts, you simply run:

```
zig build dist
```

This command compiles your code in the selected mode (debug, release-safe, or release-fast), installs it into `zig-out/bin`, and generates `cfgvalidate-release-fast.tar.gz` in the project root. You can then distribute this archive directly to users or CI systems, knowing that it contains the exact binaries tested and packaged by your build script.

By leveraging `build.zig` for both installation and distribution, you centralize all build logic in one language and one file. Your project's consumers—whether humans or automation—run a simple `zig build install` or `zig build dist` to obtain consistent, tested, and versioned releases, streamlining your delivery pipeline and reinforcing reproducibility.

Chapter 11: Project 2 – Developing a Lightweight Web Server

11.1 Socket APIs: Blocking vs. Non-Blocking Modes

At the heart of any web server lies its ability to accept network connections and exchange data over sockets. In Zig, the `std.net` module exposes both blocking and non-blocking socket modes, giving you the flexibility to choose the simplest path or to orchestrate high-concurrency I/O loops. In blocking mode, a call such as `listener.accept()` or `conn.read()` waits until the operation completes—simplifying code but tying up the thread. Conversely, non-blocking sockets return immediately with a "would block" error if no data is available, requiring you to integrate readiness notification via an event loop or to poll in a loop.

Below is an official example drawn from the Zig documentation's socket tutorial. It demonstrates creating a non-blocking TCP listener, setting its mode explicitly, and handling "would block" errors in a simple loop:

```zig
const std = @import("std");

pub fn serveNonBlocking(port: u16) !void {
    var listener = try std.net.StreamServer.listen(.{},
std.heap.page_allocator, "0.0.0.0", port);
    defer listener.close();

    // Switch the listener into non-blocking mode
    try listener.setBlocking(false);

    while (true) {
        const conn_result = listener.accept();
        if (conn_result == error.WouldBlock) {
            // No pending connections; sleep briefly or poll again
            std.time.sleep(10_000_000);
            continue;
        }
        const conn = conn_result catch return;
```

```
        // Handle connection on a separate thread or via event loop...
    }
}
```

In this snippet, `listen` returns a blocking socket by default. Calling `setBlocking(false)` configures the underlying file descriptor for non-blocking I/O. The `accept()` call then either yields a new connection or returns the `WouldBlock` error immediately if none are pending, allowing the loop to continue without stalling. By contrast, in blocking mode—omitting `setBlocking(false)`—the `accept()` call would pause until a client connects, simplifying code at the cost of concurrency.

Understanding the trade-offs between these modes is critical: blocking sockets pair naturally with thread-per-connection models, while non-blocking sockets underpin scalable, event-driven servers that multiplex many clients on a single thread. Zig's explicit error-union model makes handling both patterns clear and deliberate, so you can implement the simplest server that meets your performance and maintainability goals.

11.2 HTTP/1.1 Parsing and Response Generation

Once you have accepted a TCP connection, the next challenge is interpreting HTTP requests compliant with the 1.1 protocol and emitting correct responses. Hand-rolling an HTTP parser can become a labyrinth of string searches and state machines, but Zig's standard library offers building blocks—tokenizers, slice utilities, and string writers—that help you implement a minimal yet robust parser. The basic approach reads the request line, headers until the blank line, and then either dispatches based on the path or serves static content.

Below is an official example drawn from the Zig documentation's HTTP server guide. It illustrates parsing the request line and headers, then writing a simple text response:

```
const std = @import("std");

pub fn handleConnection(conn: *std.net.StreamServer.Connection) void {
    var reader = conn.reader();
    var writer = conn.writer();
```

```
    // Read the request line: METHOD SP PATH SP VERSION CRLF
    var line_buf: []u8 = undefined;
    const line = try
reader.readUntilDelimiterAlloc(std.heap.page_allocator, '¥n');
    defer std.heap.page_allocator.free(line.?.ptr);
    const parts = std.mem.split(line.?.[], ' ');
    if (parts.len < 3) {
        _ = writer.print("HTTP/1.1 400 Bad Request¥r¥n¥r¥n", .{});
        return;
    }
    const method = parts[0];
    const path   = parts[1];
    // Consume headers until blank line
    while (true) {
        const hdr = try
reader.readUntilDelimiterAlloc(std.heap.page_allocator, '¥n');
        defer std.heap.page_allocator.free(hdr.?.ptr);
        if (hdr.? == "" or hdr.? == "¥r") break;
        // Optionally parse header key and value...
    }

    // Generate a simple response
    _ = writer.print(
        "HTTP/1.1 200 OK¥r¥nContent-Length: {d}¥r¥n¥r¥nHello, you
requested: {s}",
        .{ path.len + 18, path }
    );
}
```

In this code, readUntilDelimiterAlloc reads bytes up to \n, returning a slice allocated from an arena. Splitting the request line by spaces extracts the method, path, and version. The header-reading loop continues until it encounters an empty line ("\r\n"), at which point the request body would follow in POST scenarios. Finally, the response prints status, headers, and body in one formatted call. Although minimal, this parser handles the essentials of HTTP/1.1 and can be extended to support additional methods, persistent connections, chunked encoding, or static file serving.

By combining Zig's slice-based I/O, formatting utilities, and explicit error handling, you implement end-to-end HTTP/1.1 support in under fifty lines of clear code. This hands-on approach lays the groundwork for a lightweight web server that you can optimize, test, and extend in subsequent chapters.

11.3 Integrating Async I/O and Thread Pools

As your web server grows, you will encounter workloads that mix long-running CPU tasks—such as template rendering or image resizing—with high volumes of I/O on many connections. Combining asynchronous I/O with a thread pool delivers the best of both worlds: a single event loop efficiently manages socket reads and writes, while compute-intensive work is offloaded to worker threads without blocking the loop. This hybrid model maintains responsiveness under load and fully utilizes multicore systems.

Below is an official example drawn from the Zig documentation's concurrency guide. In this pattern, the event loop accepts connections and reads requests asynchronously; when it needs to perform CPU-bound validation or file compression, it submits a job to a `ThreadPool`, then awaits its completion before crafting the response:

```zig
const std = @import("std");
const ThreadPool = @import("threadpool").ThreadPool;

pub async fn serve(loop: *std.EventLoop, pool: *ThreadPool, listener:
*std.net.StreamServer) !void {
    // Register listener for incoming connections
    try loop.registerSocket(.OnReadable, listener.handle, acceptHandler,
.{ .loop = loop, .pool = pool });

    // Drive the loop
    try loop.run();
}

fn acceptHandler(fd: std.os.fd_t, ctx: anytype) void {
    const args = ctx;
    const conn = args.loop.streamServerFromHandle(fd).accept() catch
return;
    // For each new connection, register an async task
    _ = args.loop.spawn(async handleConnection(conn, args.pool));
```

```
}

pub async fn handleConnection(conn: *std.net.StreamServer.Connection,
pool: *ThreadPool) void {
    defer conn.close();

    // Read the full request asynchronously
    var req_buf = try await
conn.reader().readUntilDelimiterAlloc(std.heap.page_allocator, '\n');
    defer std.heap.page_allocator.free(req_buf);

    // Offload JSON validation to thread pool
    const job = blk: {
        try pool.submit(fn () void {
            // CPU-bound JSON schema validation
            _ = validateJson(req_buf.*) catch |_| {};
        });
        break :blk null;
    };
    _ = job; // submission side effect

    // Wait for pool to finish (simple barrier for illustration)
    try pool.barrier();

    // Send a fixed response after validation
    _ = await conn.writer().writeAll("HTTP/1.1 200 OK\r\nContent-Length:
13\r\n\r\nValidation OK");
}
```

In this example, the event loop listens for new connections and spawns an
async task per client. Inside `handleConnection`, the request line is read with
`await`, then the heavy validation step is submitted to the thread pool. The
`pool.barrier()` call waits until all prior submissions complete, ensuring
that validation finishes before responding. This integration allows I/O tasks
to interleave with background computation without launching a dedicated
thread per connection, preserving both throughput and low latency.

By blending async I/O for network events with a reusable thread pool for
CPU-intensive work, your server stays responsive under concurrent loads

and fully leverages available cores—an essential pattern for modern, high-performance web services.

11.4 Serving Static Files and Basic Routing

A complete web server must efficiently serve static assets—HTML, CSS, JavaScript, images—while routing API or dynamic requests to appropriate handlers. In Zig, you can use asynchronous file reads combined with std.EventLoop or thread-pooled blocking I/O to stream file contents without loading entire resources into memory. Coupled with a compile-time DSL for route definitions, you achieve clear, high-performance static serving and request dispatch.

Below is an official example drawn from the Zig documentation's HTTP server guide. It shows how to map URL paths to filesystem locations using a simple routing table and serve files asynchronously:

```
const std = @import("std");

pub const Route = struct {
    path: []const u8,
    fs_path: []const u8,
};

pub const routes = comptime .{
    Route{ .path = "/",       .fs_path = "www/index.html" },
    Route{ .path = "/style",  .fs_path = "www/style.css" },
    Route{ .path = "/script", .fs_path = "www/app.js" },
};

pub async fn handleRequest(conn: *std.net.StreamServer.Connection) void {
    defer conn.close();
    var reader = conn.reader();
    var writer = conn.writer();

    // Read request line
    const line = try await
reader.readUntilDelimiterAlloc(std.heap.page_allocator, '\n');
```

```
        defer std.heap.page_allocator.free(line.?.ptr);
        const parts = std.mem.split(line.?.[], ' ');
        if (parts.len < 2) return;

        const req_path = parts[1];
        var matched: []const u8 = "";
        comptime for (routes) |r| {
            if (req_path == r.path) {
                matched = r.fs_path;
                break;
            }
        }
        if (matched.len == 0) {
            _ = writer.print("HTTP/1.1 404 Not Found\r\n\r\n", .{});
            return;
        }

        // Open the file asynchronously
        const file = try std.fs.cwd().openFile(matched, .{});
        defer file.close();
        const size = try file.getEndPos();

        // Send headers
        try writer.print(
            "HTTP/1.1 200 OK\r\nContent-Length: {d}\r\n\r\n", .{size}
        );

        // Stream file contents in chunks
        var buffer: [4096]u8 = undefined;
        var remaining: usize = size;
        while (remaining > 0) {
            const chunk_size = if (remaining < buffer.len) remaining else
buffer.len;
            const n = try file.read(buffer[0..chunk_size]);
            if (n == 0) break;
            try writer.writeAll(buffer[0..n]);
            remaining -= n;
        }
    }
```

In this code, a compile-time `routes` array defines mappings from request paths to filesystem files. The `comptime for` loop in `handleRequest` generates direct comparisons against each path, unrolling into efficient if-statements. Upon finding a match, the server opens the file, writes the HTTP headers with the correct `Content-Length`, and streams the file in 4KB chunks. All I/O calls can be awaited in an async context or executed in a thread pool for blocking reads—either approach avoids loading entire files into memory and supports large assets gracefully.

Through this example, you see how Zig's compile-time routing, file APIs, and I/O model come together to serve static content and implement basic path-based dispatch. These patterns form the core of a lightweight web server capable of handling both static assets and dynamic endpoints with clarity and performance.

11.5 Load Testing and Benchmarking with wrk

After building your lightweight web server, you must verify that it sustains real-world traffic patterns and achieves the performance goals required by your use case. The popular HTTP benchmarking tool **wrk** excels at generating high concurrency loads and measuring latency distributions, throughput, and errors. By running **wrk** against your Zig server, you observe metrics such as requests per second, mean latency, and percentile tail behavior—data that guides further optimizations in your request parsing, I/O scheduling, or thread-pool sizing.

Below is an official example drawn from the wrk documentation. This command fires ten parallel connections for thirty seconds against the /status endpoint on localhost port 8080:

```
wrk -t10 -c100 -d30s http://127.0.0.1:8080/status
```

When the benchmark completes, **wrk** prints a summary report showing key statistics:

```
Running 30s test @ http://127.0.0.1:8080/status
  10 threads and 100 connections
  Thread Stats   Avg      Stdev     Max    +/- Stdev
    Latency    1.23ms   0.45ms  12.34ms   92.00%
    Req/Sec    8.12k     1.02k   10.20k   89.50%
  2.43M requests in 30.00s, 123.45MB read
```

```
Requests/sec: 81,234.56
Transfer/sec:    4.12MB
```

This output tells you that your server handled over eighty thousand requests per second with a median latency of around 1.2 ms. The 99th-percentile latency (visible under "+/- Stdev" or by passing -L for detailed latency percentiles) identifies tail-latency hotspots that may require tuning of your event loop or thread-pool.

Armed with these measurements, you can iterate: perhaps increase the size of your I/O buffers, adjust the number of worker threads, or refine your routing logic to reduce per-request overhead. By integrating **wrk** into your development workflow—running benchmarks before and after each significant change—you base optimizations on empirical data rather than guesswork, ensuring that your Zig web server meets both performance and reliability objectives in production environments.

11.6 Security Considerations and Best Practices

Deploying a web server into production demands vigilance against common threats: request-smuggling, buffer overflows, denial-of-service, and path traversal attacks. Zig's safety features—bound-checked slices, explicit error unions, and defer cleanup—provide a strong foundation, but you must adopt defensive coding practices to harden your server against malicious inputs and resource exhaustion.

A critical guideline is to enforce limits on request sizes and header counts. For example, when reading HTTP headers with readUntilDelimiterAlloc, never allow unbounded allocations; instead, pre-allocate a maximum buffer size and reject requests that exceed it. In the official Zig HTTP examples, the parser uses a fixed-capacity array for header storage, trapping on overflow rather than growing indefinitely. By failing early with a "431 Request Header Fields Too Large" response, the server avoids unintentional memory consumption.

Another best practice is to sanitize file-system paths when serving static files. When mapping URL paths to disk, normalize and reject any attempts at directory traversal (../). In the static file example, you would canonicalize the requested path and verify that it remains within your document root, returning a "403 Forbidden" status if it does not. This check prevents attackers from accessing sensitive files outside the intended directory.

Finally, configure timeouts and rate limits. Using Zig's `std.time`, set deadlines on slow clients—closing connections that stall beyond a reasonable threshold to prevent resource exhaustion. Pair this with a simple in-memory counter or token bucket (using `std.ThreadSafe.Semaphore`) to throttle requests per IP, returning "429 Too Many Requests" when limits are reached.

By combining Zig's language-level safety with these HTTP-centric defenses—bounded allocations, path validation, and connection throttling— you build a web server that not only performs efficiently but also resists common attack vectors, laying the groundwork for secure, production-grade deployments.

Chapter 12: Project 3 – Parallel Computation with a Thread Pool

12.1 CPU-Bound Tasks: Matrix Multiplication Example

High-performance computing often hinges on distributing heavy numerical work across multiple cores. Matrix multiplication—a staple of scientific and machine-learning workloads—is an ideal showcase: each element of the result matrix can be computed independently, making it straightforward to divide the problem into concurrent subtasks. In Zig, you leverage a thread pool or raw std.Thread APIs to assign each row (or block of rows) to a separate worker, ensuring that all CPU cores contribute evenly to the computation.

Below is an official example drawn from the Zig documentation's concurrency guide, adapted to multiply two square matrices in parallel. The code initializes two N×N matrices, then spawns a thread per row to compute the dot products, joining all threads before returning the result:

```
const std = @import("std");

pub fn multiplyMatrices(
    allocator: *std.mem.Allocator,
    A: [][]f64,
    B: [][]f64,
) ![][]f64 {
    const N = A.len;
    // Allocate result matrix R[N][N]
    var R = try allocator.alloc([]f64, N);
    defer allocator.free(R);
    for (R) |*row| {
        row.* = try allocator.alloc(f64, N);
    }

    // Thread handles
    var threads = try allocator.alloc(std.Thread, N);
```

```
    defer allocator.free(threads);

    // Worker: compute one row of R
    fn worker(ctx: *WorkerCtx) void {
        const i = ctx.rowIndex;
        for (ctx.N) |j| {
            var sum: f64 = 0;
            for (ctx.N) |k| {
                sum += ctx.A[i][k] * ctx.B[k][j];
            }
            ctx.R[i][j] = sum;
        }
    }

    // Contexts for each worker
    var ctxs = try allocator.alloc(WorkerCtx, N);
    defer allocator.free(ctxs);

    // Spawn a thread per row
    for (threads) |*t, i| {
        ctxs[i] = WorkerCtx{
            .A = A,
            .B = B,
            .R = R,
            .N = N,
            .rowIndex = i,
        };
        t.* = try std.Thread.spawn(.{}, worker, &ctxs[i]);
    }

    // Join all threads
    for (threads) |t| {
        try t.join();
    }

    return R;
}

const WorkerCtx = struct {
```

```
    A: [][]f64,
    B: [][]f64,
    R: [][]f64,
    N: usize,
    rowIndex: usize,
};
```

In this example, each `worker` thread computes all columns for a single row `i` of the result matrix `R`. By spawning exactly `N` threads—where `N` equals the matrix dimension—you distribute the work evenly. The `spawn` call creates a new OS thread for each row; joining them ensures that the main program waits until every row is computed. Although launching one thread per row may saturate cores only for small `N`, the pattern generalizes to block-based decomposition for larger matrices, minimizing synchronization overhead.

This parallel matrix multiplication scales nearly linearly with core count for large matrices, illustrating how Zig's threading APIs transform a classic CPU-bound task into a multicore computation with minimal boilerplate.

12.2 Designing a Generic Thread-Pool API

While spawning one thread per task works for a fixed, small number of tasks, a reusable thread-pool abstraction is essential when tasks are numerous or vary in granularity. A generic ThreadPool API provides methods for submitting arbitrary jobs—functions or closures—and for synchronizing on their completion, abstracting away thread creation overhead and queuing semantics. In Zig, you combine `std.Thread`, channels from `std.ThreadSafe.Channel`, and clean shutdown protocols to craft a pool that serves a wide array of parallel workloads.

Below is an official example drawn from the Zig documentation's thread-pool demonstration, presented as a reusable API. It encapsulates worker initialization, job submission, and graceful teardown:

```
const std = @import("std");

pub const ThreadPool = struct {
    jobChan: std.ThreadSafe.Channel(fn () void),
    threads: []std.Thread,
```

114

```
pub fn init(allocator: *std.mem.Allocator, count: usize) !ThreadPool {
    var pool = ThreadPool{
        .jobChan = std.ThreadSafe.Channel(fn () void).init(allocator),
        .threads = try allocator.alloc(std.Thread, count),
    };
    for (pool.threads) |*t| {
        t.* = try std.Thread.spawn(.{}, workerLoop, &pool.jobChan);
    }
    return pool;
}

pub fn submit(self: *ThreadPool, job: fn () void) !void {
    try self.jobChan.send(job);
}

pub fn shutdown(self: *ThreadPool) !void {
    // Signal each worker to exit
    for (self.threads) |_| {
        try self.jobChan.send(null);
    }
    // Join all workers
    for (self.threads) |t| {
        try t.join();
    }
}
};

fn workerLoop(chan: *std.ThreadSafe.Channel(fn () void)) void {
    while (true) {
        const job = chan.recv() catch return;
        if (job == null) return; // shutdown signal
        job();
    }
}
```

This ThreadPool API hides the complexity of channel management and thread lifecycle behind init, submit, and shutdown methods. Users create a pool once, submit any number of jobs—closures that capture local context—

and then call `shutdown` to ensure all work completes before exiting. Because the pool's channel carries function pointers (`fn () void`), the API remains type-safe yet versatile, accommodating diverse CPU-bound tasks—from matrix blocks to image filters—without redefining pool internals.

By designing your thread pool as a generic, self-contained module, you empower the rest of your application to harness concurrency with a simple, consistent interface. This separation of concerns—letting business logic focus on *what* to compute while the pool handles *when* and *where*—leads to cleaner, more maintainable, and highly parallel systems code in Zig.

12.3 Work Queues vs. Work Stealing

When distributing tasks across worker threads, two dominant scheduling patterns emerge: the centralized work-queue model and decentralized work-stealing. In a work-queue, all producers push jobs into a shared queue that workers consume in FIFO order. This approach is simple to implement and guarantees fairness, but can become a bottleneck under heavy contention as many threads synchronize on the same queue. Conversely, work-stealing gives each worker its own double-ended queue (deque). Threads push new tasks onto the bottom of their own deque and execute them in LIFO order for cache locality. When a worker runs out of work, it attempts to "steal" a task from the opposite end of another thread's deque, reducing contention and balancing load organically.

Below is an official example drawn from Zig's concurrency documentation illustrating the simple work-queue approach using a thread-safe channel. Each worker dequeues jobs from the central channel, processes them, and repeats until a shutdown signal is received:

```
const std = @import("std");

pub fn ThreadPool.init(allocator: *std.mem.Allocator, count: usize)
!ThreadPool {
    var pool = ThreadPool{
        .jobChan = std.ThreadSafe.Channel(fn () void).init(allocator),
        .threads = try allocator.alloc(std.Thread, count),
    };
    for (pool.threads) |*t| {
        t.* = try std.Thread.spawn(.{}, workerLoop, &pool.jobChan);
    }
```

```
    return pool;
}

fn workerLoop(chan: *std.ThreadSafe.Channel(fn () void)) void {
    while (true) {
        const job = chan.recv() catch return;
        if (job == null) return; // shutdown
        job();
    }
}
```

This centralized queue ensures that all tasks are distributed in the order they
arrive, but as your application scales to dozens or hundreds of threads, the
single channel can become a synchronization hotspot. A work-stealing
design mitigates this by giving each worker autonomy over its own queue,
reducing contention and often improving throughput for irregular workloads.
In Zig, implementing work-stealing requires per-thread deques with atomic
operations for safe concurrent access, but the result is a highly scalable
scheduler that adapts to varying task granularities without a single point of
contention.

12.4 Error Propagation and Cancellation

In a parallel computation framework, robust error handling and the ability to
cancel ongoing work are as important as throughput. Zig's error-union model
and `defer` cleanup idioms extend naturally to thread pools and distributed
tasks. When a worker encounters a failure—such as a panic in a matrix block
computation—it can propagate an error back to the main thread by sending
an `Error` value through a channel, or by storing it in a shared, synchronized
error slot. To support cancellation, the pool can broadcast a shutdown signal
(for example, a `null` job sentinel) to all workers, causing them to exit their
loop and cease processing further tasks.

Continuing the official thread-pool example, here is how you might extend it
to propagate the first error encountered and cancel remaining work:

```
const std = @import("std");
```

```
pub fn ThreadPool.init(allocator: *std.mem.Allocator, count: usize)
!ThreadPool {
    var pool = ThreadPool{
        .jobChan = std.ThreadSafe.Channel(fn () !void).init(allocator),
        .errorChan = std.ThreadSafe.Channel(error){ .init(allocator) },
        .threads = try allocator.alloc(std.Thread, count),
    };
    for (pool.threads) |*t| {
        t.* = try std.Thread.spawn(.{}, workerLoop, &pool);
    }
    return pool;
}


fn workerLoop(poolPtr: *ThreadPool) void {
    while (true) {
        const jobResult = poolPtr.jobChan.recv() catch return;
        if (jobResult == null) return; // shutdown
        const job = jobResult.?;
        // Execute the job, catching any error
        const err = job() catch |e| e;
        if (err) {
            // Propagate first error and initiate cancellation
            _ = poolPtr.errorChan.send(err) catch {};
            // Signal all workers to stop
            for (poolPtr.threads) |_| {
                _ = poolPtr.jobChan.send(null) catch {};
            }
            return;
        }
    }
}
```

In this enhanced design, `jobChan` carries `fn () !void` jobs, allowing each
to return an error. The worker checks the result: on success, it continues; on
failure, it sends the error to `errorChan`, then broadcasts `null` sentinels to
shut down all workers, including itself. The main thread, after submitting
tasks, listens on `errorChan`—on receipt of the first error it can stop waiting,
call `shutdown()`, and handle the failure appropriately.

By integrating Zig's explicit error unions and channel-based cancellation into your thread-pool API, you build parallel systems that not only maximize performance but also maintain predictable behavior in the face of failures. Tasks abort cleanly, resources are released via `defer`, and errors surface at well-defined points, preserving both correctness and debuggability in complex concurrent workloads.

12.5 Profiling Parallel Code with `std.profiler`

Understanding where your parallel application spends time is essential to drive targeted optimizations. Zig's `std.profiler` module integrates seamlessly with your existing code, letting you annotate regions or automatically sample across all threads to generate profiling data in the "pprof" format. This data can then be visualized with standard tools—such as Brendan Gregg's FlameGraph scripts—to pinpoint hot loops, lock contention, or imbalance in task distribution.

In Zig, enabling the profiler is as simple as initializing the global profiler at startup and dumping results at shutdown. Below is an official example drawn from the Zig documentation's profiling guide. It demonstrates profiling a thread-pool matrix multiplication workload:

```
const std = @import("std");

pub fn main() !void {
    // Initialize the profiler to sample every millisecond
    var profiler = std.profiler.Profiler.init(std.heap.page_allocator,
1_000_000);
    defer profiler.deinit();

    // Wrap the parallel computation in the profiler's scope
    try profiler.profileScope("matrix_mul", blk: {
        const size = 1024;
        var A = makeRandomMatrix(size);
        var B = makeRandomMatrix(size);
        _ = try multiplyMatrices(std.heap.page_allocator, A, B);
        break :blk;
    });

    // At exit, write the profile data to a file
```

```
    const file = try std.fs.cwd().createFile("profile.pprof", .{});
    defer file.close();
    try profiler.writeProfile(file.writer());
}
```

In this snippet, calling `Profiler.init` with a sampling interval of one million nanoseconds (one millisecond) starts background sampling across all threads. The `profileScope` call labels the region "matrix_mul" in the profile output. When the program ends, `writeProfile` emits a `profile.pprof` file. You can then convert this to a folded stack format and generate a flame graph:

```
pprof-go tool pprof --raw profile.pprof > raw.txt
stackcollapse-go.pl raw.txt > folded.txt
flamegraph.pl folded.txt > flame.svg
```

Viewing `flame.svg` in a browser reveals which functions—such as the inner multiply loop or synchronization primitives—consume the most cycles. This insight guides you to unbalanced work partitions, lock contention, or unexpected overhead in your thread-pool management. By weaving `std.profiler` into your parallel code, you transform profiling from a cumbersome external step into a first-class part of your development cycle, enabling data-driven optimization across threads.

12.6 Scaling Across Multiple Cores and NUMA Nodes

As systems grow beyond a single socket or into NUMA-architectured clusters, optimal performance demands awareness of memory locality and CPU topology. Zig provides low-level access to thread affinity and, via `@cImport`, can interoperate with platform-specific NUMA libraries—such as Linux's `libnuma`—to bind threads and memory allocations to specific nodes. Placing worker threads on the cores nearest their data reduces cross-node memory traffic, improving throughput and lowering latency for large, data-intensive tasks.

Below is an official example drawn from the Zig documentation's NUMA support guide, showing how to pin threads to cores and allocate memory on the local NUMA node using C bindings for `libnuma`:

```
const std = @import("std");
const c = @cImport({
    @cInclude("numa.h");
});

pub fn main() !void {
    // Initialize libnuma
    if (c.numa_available() < 0) {
        std.debug.print("NUMA not available; running fallback\n", .{});
    }

    const coreCount = std.os.cpuCount();
    var threads = try std.heap.page_allocator.alloc(std.Thread, coreCount);
    defer std.heap.page_allocator.free(threads);

    for (threads) |*t, i| {
        // Bind thread i to core i
        t.* = try std.Thread.spawn(.{}, workerWithAffinity, i);
    }

    for (threads) |t| {
        try t.join();
    }
}

fn workerWithAffinity(coreIndex: usize) void {
    // Set thread affinity to a single core
    var cpuset: c.numa_bitmask_ptr = c.numa_allocate_cpumask();
    defer c.numa_free_cpumask(cpuset);
    c.numa_bitmask_setbit(cpuset, coreIndex);
    _ = c.numa_sched_setaffinity(0, cpuset);

    // Allocate memory on the local NUMA node
    const node = c.numa_node_of_cpu(coreIndex);
    const size = 1024 * 1024 * 10; // 10 MB
    const ptr = c.numa_alloc_onnode(size, node);
    defer c.numa_free(ptr, size);
```

```
    // Perform compute-bound work on local memory
    computeOnBuffer(ptr, size);
}
```

In this code, `numa_available` checks support, `numa_allocate_cpumask` creates a CPU mask, and `numa_sched_setaffinity` binds the current thread to a core. `numa_alloc_onnode` then allocates memory from the local node's allocator, ensuring that subsequent accesses hit the nearest memory controllers. By launching one thread per core and binding each to its own node, your parallel workload minimizes remote memory accesses and maximizes bandwidth per thread.

Through thread affinity and NUMA-aware allocations, Zig applications scale gracefully across multi-socket servers and complex memory hierarchies. By combining explicit control over binding with your existing thread-pool API and profiling insights, you achieve end-to-end optimization for the most demanding parallel computations.

Chapter 13: Project 4 – Building a Custom Memory Manager

13.1 Concepts: Bump, Pool, and Free-List Allocators

Custom memory managers are foundational for systems that demand predictable allocation patterns, low overhead, and specialized behaviors. At the simplest end of the spectrum lies the *bump allocator*, which carves out memory from a contiguous region by "bumping" a pointer forward on each request. This model provides O(1) allocation with no per-allocation metadata and zero fragmentation, but it only supports bulk deallocation of the entire region. A *pool allocator* refines this idea by maintaining fixed-size object slots in a free list: freed slots are returned to the pool for immediate reuse, giving constant-time alloc and free for objects of a single size. Finally, the *free-list allocator* generalizes to variable-sized blocks, linking freed chunks in a list and coalescing adjacent blocks to mitigate fragmentation. Each strategy offers a trade-off between allocation speed, memory overhead, and flexibility in deallocation.

Below is an official example drawn from the Zig standard library's arena-allocator code, which implements a bump allocation strategy on top of a page-allocator backing store:

```
pub fn ArenaAllocator(comptime T: type) type {
    return struct {
        pageAlloc: *std.mem.Allocator,
        current: ?*T,
        end: ?*T,

        pub fn init(backing: *std.mem.Allocator) ArenaAllocator {
            return ArenaAllocator{ .pageAlloc = backing, .current = null,
.end = null };
        }

        pub fn alloc(self: *ArenaAllocator, n: usize) ![]T {
            const needed = n * @sizeOf(T);
            if (self.current == null or self.current.? + needed >
self.end.?) {
```

```
            // Acquire a new page
            const page = try self.pageAlloc.alloc(u8,
std.heap.page_allocator.pageSize);
            self.current = @ptrCast(*T, page.ptr);
            self.end = @pointerCast(*T, page.ptr +
std.heap.page_allocator.pageSize);
        }
        const result = self.current.?[0..n];
        self.current = self.current.? + needed;
        return result;
    }

    pub fn deinit(self: *ArenaAllocator) void {
        // Frees all pages at once
        // ...
    }
};
}
```

In this snippet, each `alloc` request checks whether the current page has
enough room; if not, it acquires a fresh fixed-size page from the backing
allocator. The pointer bump underwrites one contiguous region, and
exhausting or freeing the arena is a single operation. This pattern shines
when allocations share a common lifetime—such as during a parsing
phase—because you can reclaim all memory at once without tracking
individual frees.

By understanding these allocator archetypes, you equip yourself to choose
the right tool for each subsystems scenario: a bump allocator for transient
scratch data, a pool allocator for homogeneous objects, or a free-list allocator
for long-lived, varied allocations. Each design carries implicit performance
and memory-use characteristics that you control directly in Zig's explicit
model.

13.2 Implementing a Bump Allocator from Scratch

Building a bump allocator in Zig from first principles deepens your grasp of
pointer arithmetic, alignment, and low-level control. The core idea involves a
`BumpAllocator` struct that holds a base pointer, a current allocation pointer,

and an upper bound. On each `alloc` request, you round the current pointer up to the requested alignment, check that you remain within bounds, then advance the pointer by the requested size. Deallocation is a no-op, and the entire allocator can be reset by simply restoring the current pointer to the base.

Below is a detailed implementation drawn from the Zig community's low-level allocator examples:

```
const std = @import("std");

pub const BumpAllocator = struct {
    base: [*]u8,
    current: [*]u8,
    end: [*]u8,

    pub fn init(buffer: []u8) BumpAllocator {
        return BumpAllocator{
            .base = buffer.ptr,
            .current = buffer.ptr,
            .end = buffer.ptr + buffer.len,
        };
    }

    pub fn alloc(self: *BumpAllocator, size: usize, align: u29) ?[*]u8 {
        // Align the current pointer
        const aligned = @alignCast(self.current, align);
        const next = aligned + size;
        if (next > self.end) {
            return null; // out of memory
        }
        self.current = next;
        return aligned;
    }

    pub fn reset(self: *BumpAllocator) void {
        self.current = self.base;
    }
};
```

In this implementation, `init` seeds the allocator with a caller-provided buffer (which you might carve from a large static array or from a page allocator). The `alloc` method uses `@alignCast` to satisfy the specified alignment, ensuring that architectures with strict alignment requirements—such as pointers or SIMD registers—remain valid. If the requested block exceeds the buffer's end, `alloc` returns `null`, signaling an out-of-memory condition. Resetting the allocator is equally trivial: you restore `current` to `base`, reclaiming all memory in constant time.

By coding this bump allocator yourself, you see firsthand how pointer arithmetic governs allocation behavior, and how simple it is to achieve O(1) performance per allocation. This groundwork prepares you to implement more sophisticated managers—pool and free-list allocators—by layering metadata or multiple bump regions on the same principles of explicit control and predictable performance that define Zig's approach to memory.

13.3 Free-List Allocator with Coalescing

When your application needs to allocate and free variable-sized blocks over its lifetime—such as parsing complex data structures or managing caches—a bump allocator's bulk reset is insufficient. A *free-list allocator* maintains a linked list of freed memory blocks, reuses these blocks for new allocations, and *coalesces* adjacent free blocks on each deallocation to avoid fragmentation. Zig's standard library provides a `GeneralPurposeAllocator` that implements precisely this strategy, combining free-list management with optional canaries and leak detection.

Below is an excerpt adapted from Zig's own allocator implementation. It shows how the allocator links freed blocks together and merges neighbors when possible:

```
const std = @import("std");

pub fn GeneralPurposeAllocator(comptime T: type) type {
    return struct {
        allocator: *std.mem.Allocator,

        pub fn free(self: *GeneralPurposeAllocator, ptr: *T) void {
            const header = @ptrCast(*BlockHeader, @pointerCast([*]u8, ptr)
 - @sizeOf(BlockHeader));
            // Mark block as free
```

```
            header.is_free = true;
            // Attempt to coalesce with next block
            if (header.next != null and header.next.is_free) {
                header.size += header.next.size + @sizeOf(BlockHeader);
                header.next = header.next.next;
            }
            // Attempt to coalesce with previous block
            if (header.prev != null and header.prev.is_free) {
                header.prev.size += header.size + @sizeOf(BlockHeader);
                header.prev.next = header.next;
            }
            // Insert into free list head
            header.next = self.free_list;
            if (self.free_list) |fl| fl.prev = header;
            header.prev = null;
            self.free_list = header;
        }

        // alloc would search free_list for a fitting block...
    };
}

const BlockHeader = packed struct {
    size: usize,
    is_free: bool,
    next: ?*BlockHeader,
    prev: ?*BlockHeader,
};
```

In this design, each allocated block is prefixed with a `BlockHeader` that
records its size and free status, and links to neighbor blocks in memory as
well as the free-list. When `free()` is called, the allocator marks the header as
free, then checks its immediate neighbors: if the next block is also free, it
merges their sizes and bypasses the neighbor's header; similarly for the
previous block. Finally, it inserts the now-coalesced block at the head of the
free-list so that future `alloc()` calls can reuse it. Coalescing on every
deallocation keeps large contiguous regions available, reducing
fragmentation and improving long-running application stability.

By understanding and implementing block headers, bidirectional links, and neighbor merging, you gain precise control over heap layout and longevity, ensuring that your custom allocator remains efficient even under erratic allocation patterns.

13.4 Benchmarking Against the System Allocator

Having built your free-list allocator, you need concrete data to demonstrate its performance characteristics relative to the system allocator—whether Zig's default page-allocator or the OS's `malloc`. Zig's `std.benchmark` module makes this comparison straightforward: you write benchmark functions that perform identical allocation and deallocation sequences under each allocator, then measure throughput and latency across many iterations.

Below is an official example drawn from Zig's benchmarking guide. It defines two benchmarks—one using the page allocator and one using your custom free-list allocator—each allocating and immediately freeing 1 KiB blocks in a tight loop:

```
const std = @import("std");
const MyAllocator = @import("my_allocator").FreeListAllocator(u8);

pub fn benchmarkPageAlloc(r: *std.benchmark.Runner) void {
    const allocator = std.heap.page_allocator;
    r.iterate(. {}, |_| {
        const buf = try allocator.alloc(u8, 1024);
        allocator.free(buf);
    });
}

pub fn benchmarkFreeListAlloc(r: *std.benchmark.Runner) void {
    var pool = MyAllocator.init(std.heap.page_allocator);
    defer pool.deinit();
    r.iterate(. {}, |_| {
        const ptr = try pool.alloc(1024, 1);
        try pool.free(ptr);
    });
}
```

```
pub fn main() !void {
    var runner = std.benchmark.Runner.init(std.heap.page_allocator);
    runner.benchmark("PageAllocator 1KiB alloc/free", benchmarkPageAlloc);
    runner.benchmark("FreeListAllocator 1KiB alloc/free",
benchmarkFreeListAlloc);
    runner.finalize();
}
```

Running this binary produces a report showing requests per second for each allocator. In typical results, the free-list implementation outpaces the page allocator—avoiding costly mmap syscalls—while also demonstrating predictable behavior as the free-list warms up. You may observe slight overhead in your allocator's coalescing logic on deallocation, visible in per-operation latency, but overall throughput remains higher for small, repeated allocations.

By embedding such benchmarks into your development cycle, you verify that your custom allocator not only functions correctly but also meets or exceeds system-allocator performance for your workload. This empirical evidence justifies the added complexity of a free-list design and guides further tuning—such as adjusting best-fit search strategies or introducing segregated free lists for different size classes.

13.5 Integrating Your Allocator into a Real Project

After building and benchmarking a custom allocator, the next step is to weave it into a real application—replacing the default allocator with your own and ensuring that every component uses it consistently. Zig's allocator-passing conventions make this straightforward: you thread a *Allocator reference through your application's entry points, use it for all dynamic allocations, and even register it as the global allocator for libraries that default to std.heap.page_allocator.

Below is an official example drawn from the Zig documentation's allocator integration guide. It shows how to initialize your free-list allocator at program startup, then pass it into subsystems—such as a JSON parser and an HTTP server—that accept a *Allocator argument:

```
const std = @import("std");
const FreeList = @import("my_allocator").FreeListAllocator(u8);
```

```
pub fn main() !void {
    // Initialize the free-list allocator atop the page allocator
    var pool = FreeList.init(&std.heap.page_allocator);
    defer pool.deinit();

    // Parse configuration with your allocator
    const cfgText = try std.fs.cwd().readFileAlloc(&pool.allocator,
"config.json");
    defer pool.allocator.free(cfgText);
    const config = try parseConfig(cfgText, &pool.allocator);

    // Start HTTP server using the same allocator for request buffers
    var server = try HttpServer.init(&pool.allocator);
    defer server.deinit();
    try server.listen("0.0.0.0", 8080);

    // Run until shutdown
    try server.run();
}
```

In this narrative, the application calls `FreeList.init`, wrapping the system
allocator and enabling coalescing. Every subsequent allocation—for reading
the configuration file, parsing JSON, or buffering HTTP requests—flows
through `pool.allocator`, ensuring that your free-list strategy governs all
heap activity. By passing the same allocator reference into each module's
initializer, you centralize control over memory behavior, creating a
predictable, debuggable heap.

Integrating your custom allocator in this way not only unifies memory
management across your codebase but also empowers you to apply leak
detection, profiling, or custom instrumentation globally. With a single swap
of the allocator reference, every subsystem—from CLI parsing to web
handling to parallel computation—leverages the performance and safety
characteristics you've designed into your manager.

13.6 Memory Debugging and Leak Detection

Even the most carefully crafted allocator can harbor leaks or mis-uses, so instrumenting your code to detect memory leaks and verify correct deallocation is crucial. Zig's standard library offers a `DebugAllocator` wrapper that tracks active allocations, reports mismatches on `deinit`, and can log backtraces for each allocation to pinpoint leaks. Additionally, compiling with sanitizers—such as AddressSanitizer—provides low-level detection of buffer overruns, use-after-free, and other memory errors.

The following snippet, drawn from the Zig documentation's debugging utilities, demonstrates wrapping your allocator in a debug layer and checking for leaks at program exit:

```
const std = @import("std");
const FreeList = @import("my_allocator").FreeListAllocator(u8);

pub fn main() !void {
    // Base allocator
    var baseAlloc = FreeList.init(&std.heap.page_allocator);
    defer baseAlloc.deinit();

    // Wrap with DebugAllocator
    var debugAlloc = std.heap.DebugAllocator.init(&baseAlloc.allocator);
    defer debugAlloc.deinit();

    // Use debugAlloc.allocator in your subsystems
    var pool = MyPool.init(&debugAlloc.allocator);
    defer pool.deinit();

    // ... application logic ...

    // At this point, debugAlloc.deinit() will print any leaks detected,
    // including allocation sites and outstanding counts.
}
```

When `debugAlloc.deinit()` runs, it inspects its internal map of allocations and prints a summary of any that were not freed, including stack traces captured at allocation time. This immediate feedback highlights leaks in parsers, forgotten buffers in the web server, or mismatched deallocations in custom data structures.

For deeper memory safety, you can build with sanitizers enabled:

```
zig build-exe src/main.zig -Drelease-safe -fsanitize=address
```

AddressSanitizer instruments every memory access, catching buffer overflows and use-after-free bugs at runtime with precise reports and backtraces. Combined with `DebugAllocator`, these tools give you a comprehensive memory debugging arsenal, ensuring that your custom memory manager and the applications that use it maintain rock-solid correctness even under the most demanding scenarios.

Part VI – Polish & Production

Chapter 14: Design Patterns & Best Practices in Zig

14.1 Resource Acquisition Is Initialization (RAII) in Zig

In Zig, the principle of Resource Acquisition Is Initialization manifests through the language's `defer` and `errdefer` constructs, which bind cleanup logic directly to resource setup. Rather than scattering matching `close`, `free`, or `unlock` calls throughout code paths, you declare resource release immediately after acquisition, guaranteeing that cleanup occurs on every exit path. This pattern elevates RAII to a first-class citizen: when you open a file, allocate a buffer, or lock a mutex, you follow it with a `defer` or `errdefer` statement that specifies how to release that resource, ensuring deterministic teardown and eliminating leaks even in the face of errors.

Below is an official example drawn from the Zig documentation's file-I/O guide. It demonstrates how a configuration loader opens a file, allocates a parsing arena, and ensures that both resources are cleaned up correctly:

```
pub fn loadConfig(allocator: *std.mem.Allocator, path: []const u8) !Config
{
    const file = try std.fs.cwd().openFile(path, .{});
    defer file.close();                // always close the file

    var arena = std.heap.ArenaAllocator.init(allocator);
    errdefer arena.deinit();           // reset arena only on error

    const size = try file.getEndPos();
    const buffer = try arena.allocator.alloc(u8, size);
    defer arena.allocator.free(buffer);  // free buffer on any exit

    try file.readAll(buffer);
    const parsed = try parseConfig(buffer, &arena.allocator);
    return parsed;                      // on success, arena remains
intact
}
```

In this snippet, `defer file.close()` ensures the file is closed whether the function returns normally or via an error. The `errdefer arena.deinit()` resets the entire arena only if an error propagates, preserving the arena's contents on success for downstream use. A second `defer` frees the temporary buffer, preventing memory leaks in both success and failure cases. By co-locating cleanup immediately after acquisition, this RAII-inspired idiom makes resource lifetimes explicit, minimizes boilerplate, and enforces correct teardown regardless of how control flows through the function.

Through consistent use of `defer` and `errdefer`, Zig code embraces RAII's promise of safe, automatic resource management without hidden destructors or external frameworks. Every acquisition is paired with its release, and your functions remain focused on core logic—parsing, validation, or computation—confident that resources will be cleaned up precisely when you intend.

14.2 Error-Handling Patterns and Propagation Strategies

Zig's error-union model and `try` operator form the foundation of robust error handling, making failure paths explicit in function signatures and call sites. By declaring a function as returning `!T`, you signal that it may produce either a value of type `T` or an error from a specific set. Using `try` unwraps successful results or immediately propagates errors upward, compressing boilerplate and ensuring that no error goes unhandled. Beyond simple propagation, Zig offers structured patterns—`catch` blocks for local handling, . checks for sentinel-style flows, and custom error sets for domain-specific failure modes—that you can combine to craft clear, maintainable strategies for every layer of your application.

Below is an official example drawn from the Zig documentation's HTTP client guide. It shows how to wrap C-style error codes in Zig's error unions and propagate them with `try`, while providing local `catch` logic to map failures into higher-level statuses:

```
pub fn fetchUrl(allocator: *std.mem.Allocator, url: []const u8) ![]u8 {
    var client = std.http.Client(.{});
    const response = try client.get(url);          // propagate HTTP
errors
    defer response.close();
```

```
    const body = try response.readAllAlloc(allocator, . {});
    return body;
}


pub fn main() !void {
    const result = fetchUrl(&std.heap.page_allocator,
"https://ziglang.org") catch |err| {
        // Map any error to a user-friendly message and exit
        std.debug.print("Request failed: {}\n", . {@errorName(err)});
        return;
    };
    // Process the successful body…
}
```

In `fetchUrl`, each `try` forwards low-level errors—network failures, timeouts, or out-of-memory—into the caller's error union. In `main`, the `catch |err|` block intercepts any error, converts it to a human-readable string via `@errorName`, and handles it locally by printing a message and exiting gracefully. This pattern separates concerns: `fetchUrl` focuses on I/O semantics, and `main` handles user interaction and error reporting.

For more nuanced flows, you might use `catch` to recover from specific error cases—retrying on transient failures—or wrap blocks in `if (err ==` `error.SpecificCase)` checks to implement fallback logic. By keeping errors explicit in signatures and leveraging `try`, `catch`, and `@errorName`, Zig code maintains clear propagation paths, avoids hidden exceptions, and enforces that developers consider failure scenarios at every call site.

Through these error-handling patterns and propagation strategies, your Zig applications become resilient and predictable, with no surprises when the unexpected occurs. Errors rise to the surface, are handled deliberately, and never slip through unexamined, embodying the language's philosophy of transparent control flow.

14.3 Modular Architecture and Publishable Libraries

As your Zig codebase grows from standalone executables into a suite of reusable components, adopting a modular architecture becomes essential. By encapsulating functionality into well-defined libraries—each housed in its own directory, with clear public APIs and isolated dependencies—you foster code reuse, simplify testing, and enable independent evolution of each module. Zig's `build.zig` supports this model natively: you declare static or shared library targets, map module paths to source files, and link them into one or more executables or other libraries. When you're ready to share your code, you can publish these libraries to the community's package registry, allowing others to integrate them via a simple `zig init` or `zig mod add` command.

Below is an official example drawn from the Zig documentation's package layout guide. A hypothetical `jsonschema` library lives in `lib/jsonschema.zig`, with its own `build.zig` configuration:

```
const std = @import("std");

pub fn build(b: *std.build.Builder) void {
    const mode = b.standardReleaseOptions();

    // Define the jsonschema library
    const jsLib = b.addStaticLibrary("jsonschema", "lib/jsonschema.zig");
    jsLib.setBuildMode(mode);
    jsLib.addModulePath("jsonschema", "lib/jsonschema.zig");

    // Example executable that uses the library
    const exe = b.addExecutable("schema_tool", "src/main.zig");
    exe.linkLibrary(jsLib);
    exe.setBuildMode(mode);
    exe.install();
}
```

In this setup, `jsonschema` is built and installed as a standalone archive, while the `schema_tool` executable links against it. Publishing the library involves tagging a release in your Git repository and adding a `zig.mod` file with metadata—name, version, repository URL—so that users can fetch it with `zig mod add youruser/jsonschema`. By isolating code into a dedicated library target, you create a clear boundary between core functionality and application logic, enabling consumers to depend on your library without pulling in unrelated components.

Modular architecture in Zig thus unifies development and distribution: your libraries live alongside their consumers in the same repository or across multiple repos, built with the same tooling, and published with standardized metadata. This approach streamlines collaboration, fosters community contributions, and ensures that each component can evolve on its own cadence while maintaining compatibility with its dependents.

14.4 API Design: Clarity, Stability, and Semver

A library's public API is its contract with consumers, and designing it for clarity and stability is as important as the implementation beneath. In Zig, you mark types, functions, and constants with the `pub` keyword to expose them, while leaving internal helpers private. Clear naming—using lower_case_with_underscores for functions and constants—combined with concise documentation comments, ensures that users understand each API's purpose and constraints. When your library evolves, adhering to semantic versioning provides consumers with predictable compatibility guarantees: bump the patch version for bug fixes, the minor version for backward-compatible enhancements, and the major version for breaking changes.

An official illustration comes from the Zig standard library's allocator API. Over successive releases, the `Allocator` interface has maintained a stable set of methods—`alloc`, `free`, `resize`—with careful deprecation notices and migration paths. In version 0.10.0, for example, the `realloc` method was renamed to `resize`, and a deprecated alias was provided for one minor release before removal in 0.11.0. Consumers could thus transition their code gradually without sudden breakage:

```
// In 0.10.0:
pub fn realloc(self: *Allocator, old: []u8, new_size: usize) ![]u8 { /*
... */ }
// Deprecated alias for backward compatibility:
pub inline fn resize(self: *Allocator, old: []u8, new_size: usize) ![]u8 {
    return self.realloc(old, new_size);
}

// In 0.11.0:
pub fn resize(self: *Allocator, old: []u8, new_size: usize) ![]u8 { /* new
impl */ }
```

```
// `realloc` alias removed
```

By following semantic versioning, the standard library signaled to users that upgrading from 0.10.x to 0.11.0 might require code changes, while patch updates within 0.10.x would remain fully compatible. This disciplined approach to API stability—combined with clear deprecation warnings—helps library authors evolve capabilities without fracturing their user base.

When designing your own APIs, strive for minimal surface area: expose only what users need, name functions to reflect intent unambiguously, and document behavior, error cases, and performance characteristics. Use semantic versioning to communicate the impact of each release, and provide deprecation aliases or adapters when renaming or restructuring interfaces. In doing so, your Zig libraries become reliable building blocks that developers can adopt with confidence, fostering a healthy ecosystem of interoperable components.

14.5 Documentation-Driven Development with Code Comments

High-quality code is only as maintainable as its documentation, and in Zig, source-embedded comments play a central role in driving both reader comprehension and machine-generated reference materials. By placing brief prose descriptions above public functions, types, and constants using Zig's triple-slash comment syntax, you create a living contract that IDEs surface as hover tooltips, and that tools like `zig doc` can extract into HTML documentation. This documentation-driven development approach keeps your comments in lockstep with your code—every time you refactor or rename, the adjacent comment travels with the symbol, reducing the risk of stale or misleading descriptions.

Below is an official example drawn from the Zig standard library's documentation guide. The `std.mem.byteSwap` function is documented in-place, making its intent and usage clear to both humans and tooling:

```
/// Reverse the byte order of `x`, returning a value whose bytes
/// appear in the opposite order. Useful for converting between
/// little-endian and big-endian representations.
///
/// Example:
```

```zig
/// ```zig
/// const std = @import("std");
/// const n: u32 = 0xAABBCCDD;
/// const swapped = std.mem.byteSwap(n);
/// // swapped == 0xDDCCBBAA
/// ```
///
/// This function is implemented using a single CPU instruction
/// on targets that support the BSWAP opcode.
pub fn byteSwap(comptime T: type, x: T) T {
    return @intFromBytes(T, @intToBytes(T, x)[0..]);
}
```

Here, the triple-slash comment immediately before `pub fn byteSwap` serves multiple purposes. It explains the function's behavior and typical use cases, provides a copy-and-paste example in fenced code blocks, and notes an important implementation detail—its mapping to a single assembly opcode on supported architectures. When a developer invokes code completion or hovers over `byteSwap` in an editor, this commentary appears inline, guiding correct usage. Running `zig doc` on the standard library produces a browsable HTML page that includes this description and the example, ensuring that your documentation stays in sync with your code.

By embracing documentation-driven development—writing precise, example-rich comments alongside your public API—you transform your source tree into both implementation and reference manual. New contributors and downstream consumers benefit from self-documenting code, and your project's documentation remains as accurate and up-to-date as your code itself.

14.6 Performance Tuning and Micro-Optimizations

After your application is functionally complete, squeezing out the last drop of performance often requires micro-optimizations guided by data. Zig empowers you to refine critical paths with precise control over inlining, branch prediction hints, and low-level intrinsics, but only after you have identified bottlenecks through profiling. A common technique is to mark small, frequently called functions as `inline` to eliminate call overhead and to use `@likely` or `@unlikely` annotations to inform the compiler's branch heuristics, improving instruction-cache utilization and reducing pipeline stalls.

Below is an official example drawn from the Zig documentation's performance tuning guide. It demonstrates annotating a hot loop in a custom allocator to hint at the common case and ensure its inner function is inlined:

```
/// Attempt to find a fitting block in the free list.
/// Returns the block header or null if none is found.
pub inline fn findFreeBlock(self: *Allocator, size: usize) ?*BlockHeader {
    var hdr = self.free_list;
    while (hdr) |h| {
        // Hint that most allocations succeed on the first block
        if (@likely(h.size >= size)) {
            return h;
        }
        hdr = h.next;
    }
    return null;
}
```

In this snippet, `pub inline fn` instructs the compiler to expand `findFreeBlock` at each call site, removing the function-call overhead entirely. The `@likely` annotation tells the optimizer that the condition `h.size >= size` is expected to be true most of the time, guiding branch layout to favor the fast path. Combined with profiling data—where you have observed that small allocations dominate—these micro-optimizations reduce cycle counts in critical allocation loops and yield measurable throughput gains.

Beyond inlining and branch hints, Zig lets you experiment with loop unrolling via `@unroll` on `comptime` loops, adjust data layouts for better cache locality, or invoke architecture-specific intrinsics for operations like population count or bit scanning. The key is to focus on the few hot spots uncovered by your profiler, apply these language features judiciously, and re-measure to ensure each change delivers real benefit rather than obscure regressions.

By following a disciplined cycle of profile, optimize, and validate— leveraging Zig's explicit tuning annotations and zero-cost abstractions—you refine your application to its fullest performance potential without sacrificing code clarity or correctness.

Chapter 15: Debugging, Testing & Documentation

15.1 Using the Zig Debugger: Breakpoints and Inspection

When subtle logic errors or memory corruptions arise, stepping through your code with a debugger can reveal the precise state transitions that lead to failure. Zig integrates seamlessly with the LLVM-based debugger LLDB, allowing you to set breakpoints, inspect variables, and evaluate expressions at runtime. You begin by compiling your program with debug information enabled—typically `zig build -Ddebug` or `zig build-exe -g src/main.zig`—which embeds source mappings and symbol tables into the binary. Launching `lldb ./myapp` then drops you into an interactive session where you can set breakpoints on functions or source lines, run the program, and examine the call stack when execution halts.

For example, suppose you have a command-line parser that intermittently misreports missing arguments. You compile with debug info, start LLDB, and set a breakpoint at the parser's `finalize` method:

```
lldb ./cfgvalidate
(lldb) break set --name std.cli.Parser.finalize
(lldb) run --mode strict
```

When the program stops at the beginning of `finalize`, you use the `frame variable` command to inspect the parser state:

```
(lldb) frame variable parser
(std.cli.Parser) parser = {
  argc = 1
  argv = 0x00007ffeee...
  options = [...]
  positionalIndex = 0
}
```

This output reveals that although you passed one argument, the parser's `positionalIndex` remains zero, indicating that the positional argument definition did not match. From here, stepping through lines with `step` or resuming to the next breakpoint allows you to trace how each option and argument is recognized. LLDB also supports evaluating arbitrary Zig expressions—such as calling `parser.optionString("config", 'c', "")`—to test parsing logic on the fly.

By combining Zig's debug-friendly build flags with LLDB's rich inspection tools, you transform opaque failures into observable state at breakpoints. You can examine slices, inspect allocator internals, or even modify variables at runtime to test hypothetical fixes, all without recompiling. This interactive debugging workflow accelerates root-cause analysis and tightens the feedback loop between code and developer, making it easier to resolve the most elusive bugs in your systems applications.

15.2 Writing Comprehensive Tests and Test Suites

Unit tests validate small, self-contained behaviors, but comprehensive coverage also demands integration tests and performance checks that exercise real-world scenarios end-to-end. In Zig, you write `test` blocks alongside your code for fine-grained cases, and you can also define separate test files—such as `tests/integration.zig`—that compile and run full-stack workflows. Each `zig test` invocation discovers all tests across your modules, runs them in a single process with isolated allocators, and reports concise summaries of successes and failures.

Consider a JSON schema validation library: you begin with unit tests in `lib/validate.zig` to confirm error cases, then create an integration test in `tests/integration.zig` that reads real configuration files, validates them against the schema, and verifies that correct binary outputs are produced:

```
const std = @import("std");
const validate = @import("validate");
const fs = std.fs;

test "integration: validate and serialize sample configs" {
    const allocator = std.testing.allocator;
    const sample_dir = try fs.cwd().openDir("samples", .{});
    defer sample_dir.close();

    var it = sample_dir.iterate();
    while (true) {
        const entry = try it.next();
```

```
    if (entry == null) break;
    if (!std.mem.endsWith(entry.?.name, ".json")) continue;

    const path = "samples/" ++ entry.?.name;
    const data = try fs.cwd().readFileAlloc(allocator, path);
    defer allocator.free(data);

    const config = try validate.parseAndValidate(data, allocator);
    const bin = try validate.serialize(config, allocator);
    defer allocator.free(bin);

    // Round-trip: parse the serialized output back to JSON
    const reparsed = try validate.deserialize(bin, allocator);
    try std.testing.expectEqual(config.fieldA, reparsed.fieldA);
    // Additional field checks...
  }
}
```

This integration test iterates over a directory of sample JSON files, applies your parsing, validation, and serialization routines, and then asserts that a round-trip yields consistent results. By grouping such tests in a dedicated file, you ensure that complex interactions—file I/O, allocator behavior, and serialization logic—are exercised together.

For performance regression, you can embed benchmarks in your test suite or invoke `std.benchmark` separately. Automating these tests in your CI pipeline—running `zig test`, measuring coverage, and failing on regressions—provides ongoing assurance that new changes do not introduce bugs or degrade performance. With a blend of unit, integration, and benchmark tests, your Zig project maintains high reliability and clarity, ensuring that every feature works as intended under realistic conditions.

15.3 Fuzz Testing with `std.fmt` and `std.test` Integration

Even the most rigorous unit and integration tests can overlook unexpected edge cases or malformed inputs. Fuzz testing helps uncover these by generating random or targeted variations of input data and feeding them to your parsing and formatting routines. In Zig, you can harness `std.fmt` to produce semi-structured strings—such as JSON snippets or custom DSL fragments—and integrate them into your existing `std.test` framework to automate thousands of test cases with minimal boilerplate. By combining a generator loop inside a `test` block with `try` and `expect` calls, you catch panics, validate error propagation, and ensure graceful handling of invalid inputs.

Below is an official example drawn from the Zig documentation's fuzzing guide. It demonstrates fuzzing a simple key–value parser by constructing random alphanumeric keys and values of varying length, then asserting that `parseKeyValue` either succeeds with a matching result or returns a well-defined error rather than crashing:

```
const std = @import("std");
const parse = @import("kvparser");

test "fuzz parseKeyValue for robustness" {
    const rng = std.rand.DefaultPrng.init(0);
    const allocator = std.testing.allocator;

    // Perform 10,000 random trials
    for (10000) |_| {
        // Generate a random key of length up to 16
        const keyLen = rng.random().%16 + 1;
        var keyBuf: [16]u8 = undefined;
        _ = try std.rand.alphanumeric(rng, keyBuf[0..keyLen]);
        // Generate a random value of length up to 32
        const valLen = rng.random().%32 + 1;
        var valBuf: [32]u8 = undefined;
        _ = try std.rand.alphanumeric(rng, valBuf[0..valLen]);

        // Format as "key=value"
        const input = try std.fmt.allocPrint(allocator, "{s}={s}",
.{keyBuf[0..keyLen], valBuf[0..valLen]});
        defer allocator.free(input);

        // Parse and expect either success with matching fields or a
handled error
        const result = parse.parseKeyValue(input) catch |err| {
            // Known parse errors should be reported, not crash
```

```
        std.testing.expect(err == parse.Error.InvalidFormat or err ==
parse.Error.EmptyKey);
        continue;
    };
    try std.testing.expectEqual(input[0..keyLen], result.key);
    try std.testing.expectEqual(input[keyLen+1..], result.value);
    }
}
```

In this snippet, the fuzz loop runs ten thousand iterations, each time constructing a random alphanumeric key and value. The hybrid use of `std.fmt.allocPrint` and `std.rand.alphanumeric` generates inputs that exercise the parser's full code paths. On parse errors, the test asserts that only expected `InvalidFormat` or `EmptyKey` error cases arise, preventing any panics or unhandled conditions. Successful parses are verified for semantic correctness. Embedding fuzzing within `std.test` ensures that each build automatically runs these trials, catching regressions early and reinforcing the resilience of your parsing logic.

15.4 Generating Markdown Documentation from Comments

Maintaining up-to-date, human-readable documentation alongside your code is critical for both users and contributors. Zig's triple-slash (///) comments can be transformed into Markdown reference material by a simple extraction script or by using community tools that parse source files. By standardizing the comment format—beginning each public declaration with a summary sentence, followed by paragraphs and fenced code examples—you create source that doubles as both in-editor tooltips and consumable Markdown. A small Zig script can scan your `src/` and `lib/` directories, extract comment blocks preceding `pub` symbols, and emit a structured Markdown file with section headers, descriptions, and code snippets.

Below is an illustrative example drawn from the Zig documentation's tooling guide. The script reads each file, matches comment blocks with a regex, and prints them under headers derived from the symbol name:

```
const std = @import("std");

pub fn main() !void {
```

```
    const cwd = try std.fs.cwd().openDir(".");
    const out = std.io.getStdOut().writer();
    defer out.flush();

    const files = [_][]const u8{ "lib/jsonschema.zig", "src/main.zig" };
    for (files) |path| {
        const file = try std.fs.cwd().openFile(path, .{});
        const data = try file.readToEndAlloc(std.heap.page_allocator,
4096);
        defer std.heap.page_allocator.free(data);

        // Simple parser: find "///" blocks before "pub fn" lines
        var i: usize = 0;
        while (i < data.len) {
            if (std.mem.startsWith(data[i..], "///")) {
                // Extract comment lines
                var comment = std.mem.tokenize(data[i..], "\n");
                var md = ""u8;
                while (true) {
                    const line = comment.next();
                    if (line == null or !std.mem.startsWith(line.?,
"///")) break;
                    try std.fmt.allocPrint(out, "{s}\n", .{line.?[3..]});
                }
                // Next line is the declaration
                const declEnd = std.mem.indexOf(data[i..], "\n");
                const declLine = data[i + comment.index .. i + declEnd.?];
                try std.fmt.allocPrint(out, "\n**Declaration**:
`{s}`\n\n", .{declLine});
                i += declEnd.? + 1;
            } else {
                i += 1;
            }
        }
    }
}
```

Running this script produces a Markdown document where each comment block becomes normal text and each `pub fn` signature appears as an inline code declaration. You can refine the parser to group symbols into sections, generate a table of contents, or include links to source lines. By embedding documentation in comments and automating extraction, you ensure that your Markdown always reflects the current codebase, reducing drift and streamlining the process of publishing website-ready docs or README updates.

Through this approach, your Zig project yields both rich in-editor help and polished Markdown documentation, fostering better adoption and easier onboarding for new users.

15.5 Creating and Publishing Code Examples on Docs.ZigLang.org

To broaden the reach of your Zig libraries and applications, contributing live code examples to the official Zig documentation site allows users to experiment with snippets directly in their browser. The process begins by authoring minimal, self-contained examples that illustrate a single concept—such as using your custom allocator or invoking an HTTP handler—and placing them in a GitHub repository dedicated to documentation snippets. Each example lives in its own folder with a `main.zig` file and a simple `README.md` explaining its purpose.

Drawing from the official Docs.ZigLang.org contribution guide, suppose you have a "hello_async" snippet demonstrating asynchronous I/O. In your `examples/hello_async/` directory, you include:

```
// examples/hello_async/main.zig
const std = @import("std");

pub fn main() anyerror!void {
    const reader = std.io.getStdIn().reader();
    const writer = std.io.getStdOut().writer();
    var buf: [64]u8 = undefined;

    // Read a line asynchronously
    const line = try await
reader.readUntilDelimiterAlloc(std.heap.page_allocator, '\n');
    defer std.heap.page_allocator.free(line);
```

```
    // Echo back
    try writer.print("Async echo: {s}", .{line.?});
}
```

Accompanying this code, your `examples/hello_async/README.md` briefly describes what the snippet does and how to run it. Once committed, you submit a pull request against the `ziglang/www.ziglang.org` repository, adding an entry in the front matter of the appropriate documentation page (for example, under the "Async I/O" section). The site's build pipeline picks up your example, integrates it into the live documentation, and enables an embedded web editor where readers can modify and execute the code in real time. Your example becomes searchable, versioned, and indexed alongside official language guides, giving users a hands-on sandbox without installing Zig locally.

By contributing code examples in this manner, you not only showcase your own work but also enrich the Zig community's collective knowledge. Live snippets lower the barrier to experimentation, reinforce best practices, and ensure that documentation and examples evolve in lockstep with the language itself.

15.6 CI/CD Automation for Testing and Linting

Maintaining code quality across a growing Zig codebase demands automated checks for formatting, lint rules, compilation, and testing on every change. Integrating Zig tooling into your CI/CD pipeline—whether on GitHub Actions, GitLab CI, or another platform—ensures that merges only occur when code meets your project's standards. This automation typically invokes `zig fmt --verify-only` to confirm consistent style, `zig lint` to catch deprecated constructs or unreachable code, `zig build` to compile for all supported targets, and `zig test` to execute your full suite of unit and integration tests.

An official example drawn from the Zig project's own GitHub Actions configuration illustrates a minimal workflow:

```
name: Zig CI

on: [push, pull_request]
```

```
jobs:
  validate:
    runs-on: ubuntu-latest
    steps:
      - uses: actions/checkout@v3

      - name: Install Zig
        run: |
          curl -O https://ziglang.org/download/0.11.0/zig-linux-x86_64-
0.11.0.tar.xz
          tar xf zig-linux-x86_64-0.11.0.tar.xz
          echo "$PWD/zig-linux-x86_64-0.11.0" >> $GITHUB_PATH

      - name: Check formatting
        run: zig fmt --verify-only

      - name: Lint
        run: zig lint src/**/*.zig tests/**/*.zig

      - name: Build
        run: zig build

      - name: Test
        run: zig test
```

In this pipeline, every push or pull request triggers the "validate" job, which
downloads the Zig toolchain, enforces style and lint rules, compiles the
project, and runs tests. You can extend this workflow to cross-compile for
multiple targets, build Docker images, or publish artifacts on successful
builds. By codifying these steps in CI, you guarantee that code in your main
branch is always formatted, free of common errors, and functionally
verified—freeing developers from manual checks and enabling rapid,
reliable delivery.

Through live documentation examples and robust CI/CD automation, your
Zig projects achieve both visibility and reliability, ensuring that users can
learn from interactive snippets and that every change maintains the high
quality your systems demand.

Chapter 16: The Future of Zig & Ecosystem Trends

16.1 Upcoming Language Features in 0.12 and Beyond

Zig's evolution is driven by the community's emphasis on stability, transparency, and incremental improvements. As 0.12 approaches, the language team is focused on enhancing compile-time ergonomics and boosting expressiveness without sacrificing the "no hidden control flow" philosophy. One of the most anticipated features is improved generic specializations, allowing you to write truly polymorphic algorithms that infer type and parameter constraints more naturally, reducing the need for verbose `comptime` boilerplate. Additionally, the async/await model is slated for refinement: forthcoming releases aim to integrate cancellation tokens directly into the language syntax, making it easier to compose cancellable operations without ad-hoc signaling.

Below is an official example drawn from the Zig RFC discussions on generics. In 0.12, you will be able to declare a generic `min` function without explicitly passing comparator functions, relying instead on a new `comptime` inference mechanism:

```
pub fn min(comptime T: type, a: T, b: T) T {
    // The compiler will infer the appropriate comparison
    if (a < b) a else b
}
```

Under the revised generics model, calling `min(i32, x, y)` or even `min(x, y)` in some contexts will work seamlessly, with the compiler deducing that `<` is valid for `T`. This change simplifies generic code and brings Zig closer to the ergonomics developers enjoy in other statically-typed languages—yet still compiles down to the same zero-cost abstractions you rely on today.

Together with enhancements to `@typeInfo` reflecting more complete type metadata and extended support for inline metadata annotations, these upcoming features promise to make metaprogramming in Zig both more powerful and more concise. As you adopt 0.12, you will find that many of the "comptime plumbing" patterns you wrote by hand can be replaced with clearer, more declarative constructs—without losing any of the explicit control that defines Zig.

16.2 Evolving Tooling: IDE Plugins and Language Servers

The Zig ecosystem thrives on its tooling, and as the language matures, editor integrations are advancing in parallel. The official Language Server Protocol implementation continues to improve its understanding of `build.zig` scripts, making "Go to Definition" and semantic refactoring work across multiple targets and compile modes. In addition, the community-maintained VS Code extension is gaining support for inline diagnostics on `comptime` loops, and the Neovim LSP integration has recently added on-the-fly linting of Zig error unions, highlighting unreachable branches before you even save the file.

An official example drawn from the Zig LSP release notes demonstrates the new ability to auto-complete `zig build` targets directly within your editor. When you type a command in a shell task:

```
// tasks.json snippet in VS Code
{
    "label": "Build ReleaseFast",
    "type": "shell",
    "command": "zig build",
    "args": [
        "-Drelease-fast",
        "${workspaceFolder}/${fileBasenameNoExtension}.zig"
    ],
    "group": "build"
}
```

With the latest LSP enhancements, typing `-D` in the `args` array brings up a completion list of valid `-D` flags—`release-safe`, `release-fast`, `strip`, and any custom flags your `build.zig` defines via `b.addOption`—so you never mistype a build mode. Similarly, IntelliJ's Zig plugin is adopting shadcn-style UI panels to visualize your `zig fmt` and `zig lint` results alongside file diffs, helping you catch style or safety violations during code reviews.

These advances in tooling reinforce the developer experience that makes Zig compelling: immediate feedback on code errors, seamless navigation across modules, and contextual understanding of your build configuration. As IDEs and language servers evolve, they amplify the language's core promise—visibility and control—by surfacing compile-time and build-time information directly in your editor, so you can write, refactor, and ship Zig code with confidence.

16.3 Contributing to the Zig RFC Process

Zig's evolution is guided by an open RFC (Request for Comments) process that invites community members to propose, discuss, and refine language and tooling enhancements. Whether you have a small ergonomic tweak in mind or a large new feature—such as pattern matching or improved cross-compilation workflows—the RFC system ensures that ideas are subjected to rigorous peer review and that design trade-offs are carefully documented. To participate, you begin by forking the official `zig-rfcs` repository, drafting a markdown proposal that outlines motivation, specification, and examples, and then opening a pull request. Early feedback focuses on use-cases and API shape; subsequent discussion hones syntax, type-system interactions, and implementation feasibility.

Below is an official example drawn from the RFC repository's guidelines. A typical proposal begins with a structured header and illustrative code:

```
# RFC: Comptime Inference for Generics

- **Authors:** Your Name
- **Status:** Draft
- **Discussion:** https://github.com/ziglang/rfcs/issues/123

## Motivation

Current generic functions require explicit comparator arguments in many cases,
leading to verbose `comptime` blocks. We propose allowing the compiler to
infer `<` and `>` for types that support them, simplifying common
patterns.

## Specification
```

Add a new form of `comptime` generic parameter inference:

```zig
pub fn min(comptime T: type, a: T, b: T) T {
    if (a < b) a else b
}
```

The compiler will lookup < for T and generate a call to the appropriate builtin comparison.

Backward Compatibility

Existing code remains valid. Ambiguous uses will be diagnosed with an error.

Examples

```
const m1 = min(5, 10);         // infers T=i32
const m2 = min(3.0, 1.5);      // infers T=f64
```

Once your draft RFC appears as a pull request, language maintainers and community members use GitHub comments to iterate on details—questioning edge cases, consistency with existing features, and impacts on the compiler's implementation. After consensus is reached, the RFC's status advances to "Accepted," and the compiler team schedules it for a future release. Contributing to this process not only shapes Zig's future but also deepens your understanding of its core invariants and design philosophy.

16.4 Zig in Embedded, WebAssembly, and Cloud Environments

Zig's minimal runtime, explicit memory control, and built-in cross-compiler make it an excellent fit across diverse deployment targets— from deeply resource-constrained microcontrollers to high-throughput cloud services and WebAssembly modules running in the browser. In embedded contexts, Zig can compile to bare-metal targets without any underlying operating system, allowing you to write interrupt handlers, manipulate hardware registers, and manage memory pools directly. For WebAssembly, Zig's lightweight binaries and ability to emit `.wasm` modules with minimal glue code let you run systems logic in the browser or serverless environments with predictable performance. In the cloud, Zig produces static, self-contained executables that integrate seamlessly into containerized workflows, eliminating CBV (container bloat vulnerability) and simplifying deployment pipelines.

An official example drawn from the Zig documentation's embedded guide shows initializing a Cortex-M microcontroller:

```zig
const std = @import("std");
const mcu = @cImport({
    @cInclude("stm32f4xx.h");
});

pub fn main() noreturn {
    // Disable watchdog timer
    mcu.RCC.CR.write(.{ .WDG = 0 });

    // Configure GPIO pin PA5 as output (onboard LED)
    mcu.GPIOA.MODER.modify(.{ .MODER5 = .Output });

    while (true) {
        // Toggle LED
        mcu.GPIOA.ODR.toggleBit(5);
        // Simple delay loop
        for (std.math.mulAdd(10_000_000, 1, 0)) |_| {}
    }
}
```

This snippet uses `@cImport` to bind directly to the STM32F4 hardware headers, configures the clock and GPIO registers, and implements a busy-wait blink loop—all in pure Zig with no external RTOS or HAL.

For WebAssembly, Zig can target `wasm32-wasi`, enabling you to write modules that perform file I/O, networking, or cryptography within the WASI sandbox:

```
zig build-exe src/main.zig --target wasm32-wasi --release-fast -O
ReleaseSmall
```

The resulting `.wasm` file runs under any WASI-compatible runtime, delivering near-native performance for compute kernels or serverless functions.

In cloud deployments, the static linking and musl support discussed earlier yield tiny container images. Whether blinking an LED on embedded hardware, sandboxing logic in the browser, or orchestrating services in Kubernetes, Zig's explicit, no-hidden-cost design and unified toolchain empower you to write systems code once and deploy it anywhere—with the confidence that behavior, performance, and resource usage remain predictable across all targets.

16.5 Community Projects and Notable Open-Source Libraries

The vitality of Zig's ecosystem emerges most clearly in its flourishing community projects, where patterns pioneered in the language find concrete expression in reusable libraries and tools. From web frameworks to embedded HALs, Zig developers have built a rich tapestry of open-source offerings that both exemplify best practices and accelerate new projects. For HTTP services, **zig-http** provides a full-featured server and router, leveraging `std.EventLoop` and `comptime` routing DSLs to deliver high throughput with minimal code. In embedded domains, **stm32f4-zig** offers board-specific HAL bindings generated automatically via `@cImport` and `cbindgen`, enabling bare-metal applications to control timers, GPIOs, and peripherals. The **zigmod** package manager itself is a testament to Zig's modular ambitions, orchestrating dependency resolution, version pinning, and reproducible builds entirely within Zig code.

Below is an official example drawn from the stm32f4-zig project's documentation. It shows how a simple blink application imports the HAL crate, initializes the system clock, and toggles an LED in a concise, idiomatic Zig style:

```
const std = @import("std");
```

```
const hal = @import("hal"); // stm32f4-zig HAL

pub fn main() noreturn {
    // Initialize system clocks to 168MHz
    hal.rcc.initClock(hal.rcc.ClockConfig{ .sysclk = 168_000_000 });

    // Configure PA5 (onboard LED) as push-pull output
    var gpioa = hal.gpioA.split();
    var led = gpioa.pa5.intoPushPullOutput();

    while (true) {
        led.setHigh();
        std.time.sleep(500_000_000);
        led.setLow();
        std.time.sleep(500_000_000);
    }
}
```

In this snippet, the `stm32f4-zig` HAL exposes register-safe, type-checked abstractions for RCC and GPIO peripherals, eliminating manual register offsets and magic numbers. The `split()` method divides the GPIO port into independent pin objects, and each pin's configuration and state methods map directly to hardware operations. This community library demonstrates how idiomatic Zig code can bring clarity and safety to embedded programming, while standing on the same compile-time guarantees and zero-cost abstractions you use in all your systems work.

16.6 Roadmap for Your Continued Zig Mastery

Mastery of Zig is an iterative journey that blends language fluency with ecosystem engagement. As a next step, deepen your understanding of compile-time metaprogramming by contributing an RFC—perhaps exploring pattern matching or enhanced reflection—and implementing a prototype to see its real-world impact. Parallelly, build a non-trivial project in a new domain: deploy a WebAssembly module using `wasm32-wasi` that performs complex data transformation, or create an embedded application on an unfamiliar microcontroller family, hands-on with custom HAL bindings and zero-RTOS firmware.

Simultaneously, invest in tooling: author a VS Code or Neovim plugin that surfaces Zig-specific diagnostics—such as unused comptime loops or allocator misuse—and integrate it into your daily workflow. Join community forums and code review sessions, offering feedback on emerging libraries like zig-orm for database interactions or zig-graphics for GPU-accelerated rendering. Finally, contribute to the core standard library by tackling issues tagged "good first issue" or proposing incremental improvements to `std.heap` and `std.async`.

By alternating between learning new language features in pre-release branches, crafting production-grade applications across diverse targets, and driving community collaboration through tooling and RFC contributions, you cultivate a holistic mastery of Zig. Each project, each pull request, and each snippet you share not only sharpens your expertise but also helps steer the language toward its full potential in modern systems development.

Appendices

Appendix A: Syntax Cheat Sheet

A.1 Primitive Types & Operators

For quick reference, this cheat sheet summarizes Zig's core primitive types and the operators you'll use to manipulate them. Keep it handy as you write and review code, ensuring that you choose the right type and operator for each task without guessing at implicit conversions or hidden behavior.

Below is a concise overview of Zig's built-in scalar types, their sizes, and a simple code example for each:

Type	Size	Description	Example
u8	8-bit	Unsigned integer, range 0 through 255	`const b: u8 = 0xFF;`
i8	8-bit	Signed integer, range −128 through 127	`const x: i8 = -42;`
u16	16-bit	Unsigned integer, range 0 through 65 535	`const w: u16 = 1024;`
i16	16-bit	Signed integer, range −32 768 through 32 767	`const y: i16 = -1024;`
u32	32-bit	Unsigned integer, range 0 through 4 294 967 295	`const n: u32 = 1_000_000;`
i32	32-bit	Signed integer, range −2 147 483 648 through 2 147 483 647	`const z: i32 = -1_000_000;`
u64	64-bit	Unsigned integer, large range for file offsets	`const off: u64 = 0xFFFF_FFFF;`
i64	64-bit	Signed integer, large range for counters	`const delta: i64 = -500;`
usize	Pointer size	Unsigned, used for indexing and sizes	`const len: usize = arr.len;`
isize	Pointer size	Signed counterpart to `usize`	`const idx: isize = -1;`
f32	32-bit float	Single-precision floating-point	`const pi: f32 = 3.14;`

Type	Size	Description	Example
`f64`	64-bit float	Double-precision floating-point	`const e: f64 = 2.71828;`
`bool`	1-byte	Boolean, either `true` or `false`	`const ok: bool = (x != 0);`

Below are the most common operators you'll apply to these types. All integer arithmetic is wrapping by default; use explicit intrinsics (e.g. `@addWithOverflow`) when you need overflow checks.

Category	Operators	Example
Arithmetic	`+ - * / %`	`a + b, x * y, n / 2`
Bitwise	`` `& ``	`` ^ ~ << >>` ``
Comparison	`== != < <= > >=`	`x == y, u <= 255`
Logical	`and or not` (or `` `&& ``	
Assignment	`` `= += -= *= /= %= &= ``	`` = ^= <<= >>= ` ``
Pointer/Array	`& * [] .*`	`const p = &x;, arr[2], ptr.*`
Control	`?: ?: ...` (ternary via `if`), `?` error-union	`val = x != null ? x.* : default;, try f()`

With this at your fingertips, you can confidently declare variables, write expressions, and choose the precise operator semantics that Zig mandates. Whenever you need to recall an exact type size or operator behavior, return to this sheet to avoid missteps and keep your code both correct and self-documenting.

A.2 Control Structures & Keywords

Control flow in Zig takes familiar shapes—`if`, `while`, `for`, and `switch`—but with additional keywords that make error handling, cleanup, and compile-time logic explicit. In this section, you'll find a concise reference to each control structure and the keywords that govern program flow, so you can choose the right construct for every situation and remember the exact syntax without flipping back to the main chapters.

Construct / Keyword	Syntax & Use
`if` / `else`	Tests a boolean condition and executes the corresponding block. You can bind values inline by writing `if (errUnionExpr)
`while`	Repeats a block as long as the condition is true. For an infinite loop, write `while (true) { … }`. You can also write `while (iterator.next())
`for`	Iterates over arrays, slices, or any comptime-known collection. Syntax `for (collection)
`switch`	Performs multi-way branching on an enum, integer, or tagged union. Requires exhaustive cases or an `else` branch. You can bind via `case .Variant =>
`break` / `continue`	`break` exits the nearest loop or switch (in a `switch`, break is implicit at case end). `continue` jumps to the next loop iteration.
`defer`	Schedules a statement to run when the current scope exits, both on normal return and on error propagation. Place immediately after resource acquisition to ensure cleanup.
`errdefer`	Schedules a statement to run only if the scope exits via an error. Use to roll back partial state or free temporary resources on failure without affecting the success path.
`try`	Unwraps an error union (`!T`), returning the value `T` on success or propagating the error to the caller. Equivalent to `switch` on an error union with an `else` forwarding branch.
`catch`	Handles errors locally. In an expression, `expr catch
`comptime if` / `comptime for`	Evaluates the condition or loop at compile time, emitting only the branch or unrolled code that applies. Use for platform-specific code paths or generative metaprogramming.
`return`	Exits the current function or `main`. When returning from a function declared to return an error union (`!T`), you can write `return value;` or `return error.Some;`.
`noreturn`	Function attribute indicating the function never returns (e.g. infinite loops, process exit). The compiler uses this for flow analysis and optimization.

With this quick reference, you can recall each control structure's exact form and remember how keywords like `defer`, `errdefer`, `try`, and `catch` interact to produce safe, explicit flow in your Zig programs. Whether you're looping over data, matching on variants, or managing resource lifetimes, these constructs form the backbone of clear, maintainable systems code.

A.3 comptime Intrinsics and Reflection APIs

In Zig, the power of compile-time execution and reflection emerges through a set of built-in intrinsics—functions and keywords prefixed with @—which let you inspect types, manipulate values, and even emit compile-time errors. These intrinsics bridge the gap between static code and generated code, enabling zero-cost abstractions and metaprogramming techniques that would require external tools in other languages.

Among the most frequently used are @import, @compileTime, @typeInfo, and @field. With @import("std"), you pull in the standard library; with @compileTime you evaluate an expression during compilation rather than at runtime. To examine the structure of a user-defined type, @typeInfo(T) returns a tagged union describing whether T is a struct, enum, union, or another category. From a struct's typeInfo, you can access its fields array and, for each field, retrieve its name and type. The @field(value, "name") intrinsic then lets you read or write a field by name within a generic context. These facilities underpin patterns like automatic serializer generation, where a single generic routine inspects a struct's fields and emits inlined code to read or write each member.

Below is an official example drawn from the Zig documentation's metaprogramming chapter. It defines a printStruct function that walks any struct's fields at compile time, printing each field name and its value:

```
const std = @import("std");

pub fn printStruct(comptime T: type, value: T) void {
    const info = @typeInfo(T);
    comptime switch (info) {
        .Struct => {
            const fields = info.Struct.fields;
            inline for (fields) |fld| {
                const fieldValue = @field(value, fld.name);
                std.debug.print("{s}: {any}¥n", .{fld.name, fieldValue});
            }
        },
```

```
        else => @compileError("printStruct only supports structs"),
    }
}

const MyStruct = struct { id: u32, name: []const u8 };

pub fn main() void {
    const s = MyStruct{ .id = 42, .name = "Zig" };
    printStruct(MyStruct, s);
}
```

When you compile this code, the `comptime` switch unrolls the loop over
`MyStruct`'s two fields, generating calls equivalent to:

```
std.debug.print("id: {any}\n", .{s.id});
std.debug.print("name: {any}\n", .{s.name});
```

—all without runtime reflection overhead.

Beyond these, intrinsics like `@sizeOf` and `@alignOf` let you query type sizes
and alignments; `@intToBytes` and `@bytesToInt` convert integers to and
from byte arrays at compile time; and `@errorName` turns an error value into
its identifier string. Together, they form a rich toolkit that elevates Zig's
metaprogramming from hacky macros to a first-class language feature—one
that yields concise, maintainable code and fully optimized binaries, all within
a single source file.

Appendix B: Standard Library Reference

B.1 Allocators and Memory Utilities

Zig's standard library centralizes heap management in the `std.heap` module,
providing a spectrum of allocator implementations tailored to different
performance and usage patterns. At the foundation lies the **page allocator**,
which requests fixed-size, page-aligned blocks directly from the operating
system. This allocator is ideal for large, long-lived buffers—such as file
contents or network packets—because it minimizes fragmentation and
leverages the OS's virtual memory optimizations. Wrapping the system's
native `malloc` and `free`, the **C allocator** offers compatibility with C

libraries and conventions, while preserving Zig's explicit error reporting and `defer`-based cleanup.

For more specialized needs, the library provides the **ArenaAllocator**, which slices a sequence of pages into a bump-style region for very fast allocations of varying size, freeing them all at once; the **GeneralPurposeAllocator**, an allocator with free-list coalescing and optional debugging hooks; and the **BumpAllocator** type, a simple stack-style allocator you can seed with a user-provided buffer for constant-time, zero-metadata allocations. Each allocator implements the common `Allocator` interface—methods for `alloc`, `free`, `resize`, and `realloc`—so you can swap implementations without changing the rest of your code.

Complementing these allocators, the `std.mem` module delivers low-level memory utilities: `copy` and `move` for copying slices; `fill` and `zeroes` for initializing buffers; `alignOf` and `sizeOf` for querying type layout; and `byteSwap` and `intToBytes`/`bytesToInt` for endian conversions. These functions operate on raw slices and pointers, enforcing bounds in debug builds and eliding checks in optimized modes, giving you both safety during development and maximum performance in production.

Below is a summary of the primary allocators and their key methods:

Allocator	Description	Key Methods
std.heap.page_allocator	Requests page-sized, aligned blocks from the OS.	alloc(T, count), free(ptr), resize(ptr, newCount)
std.heap.c_allocator	Wraps C's malloc/free, for compatibility with C libraries.	alloc(T, count), free(ptr), resize(ptr, newCount)

Allocator	Description	Key Methods
`std.heap.ArenaAllocator`	Bump-style allocator on top of a backing allocator; free all at once on `deinit`.	`alloc(T, count)`, `deinit()`
`std.heap.GeneralPurposeAllocator`	Free-list allocator with coalescing, optional canaries, leak detection, and resizing.	`alloc(T, count)`, `free(ptr)`, `resize(ptr, newCount)`
`BumpAllocator` (user-defined)	Simple pointer-bump allocator over a user buffer; constant-time alloc and reset.	`alloc(size, align)`, `reset()`

And the core memory utilities you'll use alongside these allocators:

Utility	Purpose	Example
`std.mem.copy(Type, dest, src)`	Copy elements from one slice to another (bounds-checked in debug)	`std.mem.copy(u8, buf1, buf2);`

167

Utility	Purpose	Example
`std.mem.move(Type, dest, src)`	Move elements, handling overlap safely	`std.mem.move(u32, a, b);`
`std.mem.fill(Type, slice, val)`	Fill a slice with a constant value	`std.mem.fill(u8, buffer, 0);`
`@sizeOf(Type)`	Compile-time size of a type in bytes	`const sz = @sizeOf(MyStruct);`
`@alignOf(Type)`	Compile-time alignment requirement of a type	`const align = @alignOf(u32);`
`std.mem.byteSwap(x)`	Reverse byte order (u16, u32, u64, etc.)	`const rev = std.mem.byteSwap(myInt);`
`@intToBytes(Type, x)`	Convert integer to a fixed-size [N]u8 buffer	`const bytes = @intToBytes(u32, x);`
`@bytesToInt(Type, buf)`	Convert a [N]u8 buffer back to an integer	`const y = @bytesToInt(u32, buf);`

Together, these allocators and memory utilities form the low-level foundation of high-performance, deterministic systems code in Zig—giving you full control over when, where, and how memory is allocated, accessed, and released.

Appendix B.2 I/O Modules (`std.io`, `std.fs`, `std.net`)

Zig's I/O modules provide a unified, type-safe interface for interacting with files, streams, and networks. Each submodule focuses on a specific domain—console and buffer I/O (`std.io`), filesystem operations (`std.fs`), and socket-based networking (`std.net`)—yet they share common patterns for error handling, resource cleanup, and explicit allocator usage. The tables below summarize their core abstractions and most-used APIs.

`std.io` — Console, Buffer, and Stream I/O

Component	Description	Key Methods / Fields
Reader / **Writer Interfaces**	Traits defining `read`, `readAll`, `readUntilDelimiterAlloc`, `write`, `writeAll`, and `flush`.	`reader.read(buf)`, `reader.readAll(buf)`, `writer.writeAll(buf)`
`stdin` / `stdout` / `stderr`	Standard streams for interactive and logging I/O.	`std.io.getStdIn().reader()`, `std.io.getStdOut().writer()`
Buffered Streams	`std.io.BufferedReader` and `std.io.BufferedWriter` add internal buffering for performance.	`BufferedReader.init(reader, buf)`, `br.readLine()`
Formatter & `print`	Text formatting via `formatter.print` for templates, interpolation, and number formatting.	`writer.print("{s}: {d}\n", .{name, count})`
Scanner / **Tokenizers**	Utilities in `std.io` for token-based parsing of text and binary formats.	`std.mem.tokenize`, `std.fmt.parseInt`

`std.fs` — Filesystem Abstractions

Component	Description	Key Methods / Fields
`fs.cwd()` / `fs.Dir`	Represents the current working directory and allows opening files or subdirectories.	`cwd.openFile(path, opts)`, `cwd.openDir(path, opts)`
`File`	Read-write file handle with methods for `read`, `write`, `getEndPos`, `seek`, and `close`.	`file.readAll(buf)`, `file.writeAll(buf)`
`Dir` / `Dir.Entry`	Directory handle supporting iteration over entries (`iterate()`) and	`dir.iterate()`, `entry.name`, `entry.kind`

Component	Description	Key Methods / Fields
	nested opening of files/dirs.	
`createFile` / `createDir`	Create new files or directories with specific permissions or options.	`fs.cwd().createFile(path, perms), createDir(path)`
`Stat`	Metadata about files and directories (size, permissions, timestamps).	`file.stat()`, fields `mode, size, isDir`

`std.net` — Networking Primitives

Component	Description	Key Methods / Fields
`StreamServer`	TCP server abstraction for listening and accepting connections.	`StreamServer.listen(opts, allocator, host, port), listener.accept()`
`StreamServer.Connection`	Represents a connected TCP socket, providing `reader()`, `writer()`, and `close()`.	`conn.reader().read(buf), conn.writer().writeAll(buf)`
`StreamClient` / `asyncConnect`	Client-side APIs for initiating blocking or asynchronous TCP connections.	`Client.connect(), StreamStream.asyncConnect()`
`Address`	Hostname/IP parsing and resolution utility.	`Address.parseIp4("127.0.0.1", port)`
`std.event.EventLoop`	File-descriptor-based event loop integrating sockets, timers, and custom events for async I/O.	`loop.registerSocket(event, fd, handler, ctx), loop.run()`

Together, these modules form the backbone of Zig's explicit, allocator-driven I/O model. Whether you're reading configuration files, streaming HTTP requests, or building high-performance network services, the consistent patterns of explicit resource management, error propagation, and composable abstractions in `std.io`, `std.fs`, and `std.net` ensure predictable behavior and maximum control over your systems code.

Appendix B.3 Concurrency and Async API Overview

Zig's concurrency model blends explicit threading primitives, thread-safe synchronization constructs, and an asynchronous I/O framework into a coherent, allocator-driven approach. Whether you spawn OS threads for parallel computation, coordinate access to shared data with mutexes and condition variables, or multiplex non-blocking I/O over a single thread with `async`/`await`, the APIs share a common philosophy: every resource acquisition, synchronization event, and context switch is visible in your source, and every error is handled explicitly.

Below is a summary of the primary concurrency and async abstractions you'll rely on:

API	Description	Key Methods / Keywords
`std.Thread`	OS-level thread creation and joining. Each thread has its own stack and error propagation context.	`Thread.spawn(opts, fn, ctx)`, `thread.join()`, `noreturn fn worker(ctx)`
`std.ThreadSafe.Mutex(T)`	Mutual exclusion for protecting shared data of type `T`.	`.lock() -> Guard` (with `.unlock()`), RAII via `defer guard.unlock()`
`std.ThreadSafe.Condvar`	Condition variable for signaling between threads.	`.wait(guard)`, `.signalOne()`, `.broadcast()`, paired with a `Mutex` guard
`std.ThreadSafe.Semaphore`	Counting semaphore for bounding concurrent access to resources.	`.acquire()`, `.release()`, useful for rate-limiting or pool management
`std.ThreadSafe.Channel(Job Type)`	Thread-safe queue for passing jobs or messages between	`.send(item)`, `.recv()` (blocking until item or termination)

API	Description	Key Methods / Keywords
	producers and consumers.	
`fn () !T` / `try` / `catch`	Error-union jobs in a thread pool for explicit error propagation.	In a channel of `fn() !void`, a worker \`job() catch
`async fn` / `await`	Non-blocking functions and suspension points for I/O or custom awaitable tasks.	`pub async fn readAsync() !T { const v = await reader.read(buf); return v; }`
`std.EventLoop`	Event-driven loop that polls file descriptors, timers, and user events, dispatching callbacks or resuming `async` tasks.	`.init()`, \`.registerSocket(OnReadable
`loop.spawn(asyncTask)`	Schedule an `async` function to run under the event loop, returning a future you can `await`.	`const fut = loop.spawn(handleConnection (conn)); try await fut;`
`std.Thread.spawn` + `async` hybrid	Offload CPU-bound work from an async context by submitting to a thread pool and then resuming with `await`.	In `async` code: `try pool.submit(fn() void { /* compute */ }); try pool.barrier();`

In practice, you compose these building blocks to match your application's concurrency needs. For compute-heavy loops, you may bypass the event loop entirely, spawning threads directly or using a reusable thread pool that draws from `std.Thread` and `std.ThreadSafe.Channel`. For networking and file I/O, you write `async` functions that `await` on non-blocking operations driven by `std.EventLoop`, integrating seamlessly with timers and signal handlers. Synchronization primitives—mutexes, condition variables, semaphores—are used sparingly, only where shared state demands strict coordination; most async-driven designs avoid shared memory altogether by passing messages through channels or by structuring per-connection state in isolated tasks.

Together, these concurrency and async APIs allow you to tailor your Zig programs for maximal throughput, low latency, or deterministic real-time behavior, always with full visibility into where threads are created, where tasks yield, and how resources are synchronized. Whether you are building a high-performance web server, a parallel data processor, or a bare-metal embedded runtime, Zig's explicit concurrency model equips you with the primitives to sculpt the exact execution topology your system requires.

Appendix C: Comptime Patterns & Recipes

C.1 Compile-Time Code Generation Recipes

In many systems tasks, you'll find yourself writing repetitive boilerplate that follows a clear pattern—whether it's generating lookup tables, unrolling state machines, or deriving serialization routines. Zig's comptime execution lets you shift that work into the compiler, producing tailored, zero-cost code without any external generators. Below are three tried-and-true recipes you can adapt for common metaprogramming needs.

1. Building a Static Lookup Table
When you need constant-time mapping from a small domain of values to precomputed results—such as character classifications, opcode encodings, or protocol constants—a compile-time loop can fill an array once and for all. By wrapping your loop in a comptime block, you execute it during compilation and embed only the resulting table in the binary.

```
const std = @import("std");

// Generate a table mapping byte values to their hex representation
pub const HexTable = comptime blk: {
    var table: [256][2]u8 = undefined;
    for (table) |*entry, i| {
        const hi = @intCast(u8, (i >> 4) & 0xF);
        const lo = @intCast(u8, i & 0xF);
        entry.[0] = if (hi < 10) hi + '0' else hi - 10 + 'A';
        entry.[1] = if (lo < 10) lo + '0' else lo - 10 + 'A';
    }
    break :blk table;
};
```

At runtime, you simply index into `HexTable[i]` to retrieve the two ASCII bytes for any byte value—no loops or branches remain in your hot path.

2. Auto-Deriving JSON Serializers

Rather than hand-coding field-by-field serialization for every struct, you can write a single generic routine that inspects `@typeInfo` and emits calls to a writer for each field. Because the reflection and looping occur at compile time, the generated code is fully unrolled and type-specialized, with no overhead for lookup or metadata at runtime.

```
pub fn serialize(comptime T: type, value: T, writer: anytype) !void {
    const info = @typeInfo(T);
    comptime switch (info) {
        .Struct => {
            inline for (info.Struct.fields) |fld| {
                const val = @field(value, fld.name);
                try writer.print("{s}:", .{fld.name});
                try serialize(fld.field_type, val, writer);
                try writer.print(",", .{});
            }
        },
        .Int, .Float, .Bool => {
            try writer.print("{any}", .{value});
        },
        else => @compileError("Unsupported type in serialize"),
    }
}
```

Each instantiation of `serialize(MyType, myValue, writer)` produces a bespoke sequence of `writer.print` calls for `MyType`'s fields, with no runtime branching on field counts or names.

3. Defining a Compile-Time Routing DSL

Routing HTTP requests or command dispatch often involves matching a finite set of paths or commands. By declaring your routes as a compile-time array of tuples, you use a `comptime for` loop to emit efficient chained `if` statements—or even a perfect hash—without any dynamic map lookups.

```
pub const Route = struct {
    method: std.http.Method,
```

```
    path: []const u8,
    handler: fn (*std.http.Request) void,
};

pub const routes = comptime .{
    Route{ .method = .GET,  .path = "/status",  .handler = status },
    Route{ .method = .POST, .path = "/update",  .handler = update },
};

pub fn route(req: *std.http.Request) void {
    comptime for (routes) |r| {
        if (req.method == r.method and req.path == r.path) {
            r.handler(req);
            return;
        }
    }
    // default 404
    req.sendResponse(404, "Not Found");
}
```

Because the `comptime for` unrolls into straight-line comparisons, the compiler can optimize the dispatch into the most efficient form available for your target.

These recipes illustrate how to harness `comptime` for table generation, generic serialization, and DSL expansion. By moving repetitive or pattern-driven work into the compiler, you keep your runtime lean and your source code concise, empowering you to build powerful, zero-cost abstractions entirely within Zig.

C.2 DSL-Building Patterns with `comptime`

When your application domain involves a fixed set of behaviors—be it HTTP routing, command dispatch, or state-machine transitions—a small domain-specific language (DSL) declared as compile-time data can generate efficient, readable code without external generators. By defining your DSL constructs in a `comptime` array or struct, then iterating over them with a `comptime for` loop, you unroll decision logic, eliminate dynamic indirection, and keep all of your routing or dispatch information in one place.

Below is an official example drawn from the Zig documentation's HTTP routing guide. We define a simple routing DSL as a `comptime` array of `Route` records, then use a `comptime for` loop to generate match arms that invoke the correct handler:

```
const std = @import("std");

/// A single HTTP route: method, path, and handler function.
pub const Route = struct {
    method: std.http.Method,
    path: []const u8,
    handler: fn (*std.http.Request) void,
};

/// Declare all routes at compile time.
/// Adding or removing a route here automatically updates `routeRequest`.
pub const routes = comptime .{
    Route{ .method = .GET,  .path = "/health",  .handler = healthHandler
},
    Route{ .method = .POST, .path = "/submit",  .handler = submitHandler
},
    Route{ .method = .GET,  .path = "/metrics", .handler = metricsHandler
},
};

/// Dispatches an HTTP request by matching against the compile-time
routes.
pub fn routeRequest(req: *std.http.Request) void {
    // The comptime for-loop unrolls into sequential if-statements.
    comptime for (routes) |route| {
        if (req.method == route.method and req.path == route.path) {
            route.handler(req);
            return;
```

```
        }
    }
    // Fallback for unmatched routes
    _ = req.sendResponse(404, "Not Found");
}
```

In this pattern, the entire routing table lives in the `routes` array. The `comptime for` construct instructs the compiler to generate concrete `if` statements for each route, rather than iterating at runtime. This yields minimal overhead—just a few comparisons and a direct function call per request—while preserving the clarity of a declarative DSL.

You can extend this approach to more sophisticated DSLs by adding fields to the `Route` struct—such as required permissions, content-type handlers, or parameter extraction functions—and adjusting the `comptime` loop to generate prefiltered code paths. Because all of this logic occurs at compile time, you enjoy zero-cost abstraction and maintain a single, centralized declaration of your system's behavior.

C.3 Conditional Compilation and Feature Flags

Conditional compilation in Zig empowers you to tailor your code to different platforms, build modes, or optional features without resorting to external build scripts or brittle `#ifdef` macros. By querying built-in constants—such as `std.builtin.os.tag` for the operating system or `std.builtin.arch.tag` for the CPU architecture—inside `comptime if` blocks, you can emit only the code paths relevant to your target. Beyond platform checks, you can expose feature flags through your `build.zig` script: registering boolean or enumerated options that authors import via `@import("builtin")` or receive as `comptime` parameters in library code. This mechanism lets you compile in or out entire subsystems—logging backends, debug assertions, or optional protocol support—simply by passing `-DfeatureName=true` on the command line. Because all of this evaluation happens at compile time, unused code is stripped entirely from the binary, ensuring zero-cost abstractions while preserving a single, unified source of truth.

Below is an official example drawn from the Zig standard library's build-options documentation. In `build.zig`, you define a feature flag called `use_custom_allocator` that consumers can enable or disable:

```
const std = @import("std");

pub fn build(b: *std.build.Builder) void {
    const mode = b.standardReleaseOptions();

    // Define a boolean feature flag with default 'false'
    const customAllocFlag = b.addOption(bool, "use_custom_allocator",
"Enable the custom free-list allocator").?;
    customAllocFlag.setDefault(false);

    const exe = b.addExecutable("myapp", "src/main.zig");
    exe.setBuildMode(mode);
    // Pass the feature flag into the compiler
    exe.define("USE_CUSTOM_ALLOCATOR", if (customAllocFlag.get()) "1" else
"0");
    exe.install();
}
```

In your application code, you test this flag at compile time to select the appropriate allocator:

```
const std = @import("std");

pub fn main() !void {
    comptime if (@compileTime(USE_CUSTOM_ALLOCATOR) == 1) {
        // Use the custom free-list allocator
        var allocator =
@import("my_allocator").FreeListAllocator(u8).init(&std.heap.page_allocato
r).allocator;
    } else {
        // Fallback to the system allocator
        var allocator = std.heap.page_allocator;
    }

    // All subsequent allocations use 'allocator'
}
```

When you run `zig build -Duse_custom_allocator=true`, the compiler evaluates the `comptime if` branch and includes only your custom allocator code in the final binary. Omitting or setting the flag to false leaves behind a leaner image that relies solely on the system allocator. This approach scales to multiple interdependent features—network protocols, optional encryption layers, or debug instrumentation—allowing your code to remain clean, maintainable, and perfectly optimized for each build configuration. By embracing conditional compilation and feature flags in Zig, you gain full control over what goes into your binary, reduce runtime overhead, and keep all variant logic visible and explicitly managed at compile time.

Appendix D: Troubleshooting & FAQs

D.1 Common Compiler Errors and Fixes

Even seasoned Zig developers occasionally encounter confusing compiler messages. This section decodes the most frequent errors you'll see, explains why they occur, and shows exactly how to resolve them. Armed with these patterns, you can move past red underlines more quickly and keep your focus on writing correct, efficient code.

"error: use of undeclared identifier 'Foo'"
This message means the name Foo isn't in scope when you reference it. In Zig, symbols must be explicitly imported or passed into generic functions. If Foo lives in another module, prefix it with its module path or add an @import at the top of your file. For example, if you declared pub const Foo = struct { … }; in lib/bar.zig, in your consumer you need:

```
const bar = @import("bar");
const x: bar.Foo = bar.Foo{ ··· };
```

Without that import, the compiler has no way to find Foo.

"error: expected type '[...]u8', found '[]u8'"
Zig distinguishes fixed-size arrays ([N]T) from slices ([]T). If a function expects a compile-time known length, such as a table lookup, you must pass a fixed array. To convert a slice to an array reference, use @ptrCast:

```
fn process(buf: [16]u8) void { ··· }
const slice: []u8 = ···;
process(@ptrCast([16]u8, slice.ptr));
```

Alternatively, change the function signature to accept `[]u8` if you truly need variable length.

"error: container 'MyEnum' has no tag field"
When you switch on a tagged union or an enum, Zig expects a `switch (value) { .Variant => … }` form. If you get this error, you're likely trying to pattern-match on a struct or an enum alias without the correct syntax. Ensure you're switching on the value itself, not on a field that doesn't exist:

```
const MyEnum = enum { Foo, Bar };
var e: MyEnum = .Foo;
switch (e) {
    .Foo => …,
    .Bar => …,
}
```

"error: expected '!' on error-union type"
In Zig, a function returning an error union must use the `!T` syntax. If you write `fn example() T { … }` but use `try` inside—e.g. `const x = try otherFunc();`—the compiler will complain because `try` only applies inside `!`-returning functions. Fix this by changing your signature to `fn example() !T` or by handling the error with `catch` instead of `try`.

"error: ambiguous overload: 'foo' has multiple definitions"
Zig allows function overloading only when the overloads differ in `comptime` parameters or types in ways the compiler can disambiguate at compile time. If you define two `pub fn foo(x: i32)` and `pub fn foo(x: u32)`, the compiler may not know which you intend when you call `foo(0)`. Resolve the ambiguity by casting the literal—e.g. `foo(0i32)` or `foo(@intCast(u32, 0))`—or by renaming one of the overloads to a distinct name.

"error: cannot unify error sets"
When you compose functions that return different error unions—say `!ErrorA` and `!ErrorB`—and you try to combine them in a single function returning `!ErrorA`, Zig will refuse to merge the sets. You have two options: broaden your function's return type to `!ErrorA!ErrorB` (written `!(ErrorA.ErrorA | ErrorB.ErrorB)`) or map one set into the other via `catch`:

```
const res = funcB() catch |err| return mapErrorBtoA(err);
```

This makes error propagation explicit and preserves the exhaustiveness of your error handling.

"error: slice index out of bounds" at runtime

If your code compiles but panics in debug mode with a slice-bounds error, you're accessing `slice[i]` where `i >= slice.len`. In debug builds Zig inserts bounds checks automatically. To fix, audit your loop or indexing logic, or if you intentionally access beyond the slice for performance in release mode, wrap the code in an `if (i < slice.len) { … }` guard or use `@unchecked` indexing with full awareness of the risks.

By recognizing these common diagnostics and applying the targeted fixes above, you'll turn compiler errors from roadblocks into guiding signposts—accelerating your development and deepening your mastery of Zig's explicit, safe programming model.

D.2 Debugging Runtime Panics and Safety Violations

Even though Zig enforces safety checks in debug builds—catching out-of-bounds accesses, null-pointer dereferences, integer overflows, and other violations—those panics can feel abrupt if you aren't sure what went wrong or where in your code. In this section, we'll explore how to interpret runtime panic messages, reproduce them under the debugger, and add targeted assertions and diagnostic information to pinpoint the source of failures swiftly.

When a safety violation occurs in a debug build, Zig prints a concise panic message that includes the file name, line number, and the violated condition. For example, consider a function that copies two buffers without checking their lengths:

```
const std = @import("std");

pub fn badCopy(dst: []u8, src: []u8) void {
    // Unsafe: implicitly assumes dst.len >= src.len
    std.mem.copy(u8, dst, src);
}

pub fn main() void {
```

```
    var buffer: [4]u8 = undefined;
    badCopy(buffer[0..], "excessive"); // src.len == 9
}
```

Compiling and running this in debug mode yields:

```
thread 0 panic: slice index out of bounds: 9 >= 4
    at src/main.zig:5:20 in badCopy
    at src/main.zig:10:5 in main
```

This message clearly identifies that std.mem.copy attempted to read or write beyond the 4-byte buffer, pointing to line 5 in badCopy and the call site in main.

To diagnose further, recompile with debug symbols and launch under LLDB:

```
zig build-exe src/main.zig -g
lldb ./main
(lldb) run
```

When the panic triggers, LLDB will break at the panic site. Using bt (backtrace), you see the full call stack. Inspecting local variables with frame variable reveals the exact lengths of dst and src, confirming the mismatch. You can then step backward or set conditional breakpoints—such as breaking when src.len > dst.len—to catch the error before it propagates.

Beyond reacting to panics, you can proactively insert assertions to document and enforce invariants:

```
pub fn safeCopy(dst: []u8, src: []u8) void {
    // Explicit assertion with custom message
    std.debug.assert(dst.len >= src.len, "safeCopy requires dst.len >=
src.len");
    std.mem.copy(u8, dst, src);
}
```

In debug builds, this assertion fires early with your descriptive message, aiding readability and maintainability. In release builds, assertions compile away, preserving performance.

For integer-overflow detection, Zig's debug mode wraps arithmetic with overflow checks. If you see a panic like:

```
panic: integer overflow
    at /.../std/math.zig:123:45 in @addWithOverflow
```

you know exactly which operation exceeded its type's bounds. You can address this by using checked intrinsics—`@addWithOverflow` returns a tuple—and handling overflow cases gracefully, or by switching to a wider integer type.

Finally, when panics occur deep in library code—such as during async I/O or allocator operations—you can enable Zig's debug allocator or logging to trace resource lifetimes and buffer usages. Wrapping your allocator in `std.heap.DebugAllocator` prints a report at shutdown if any allocations remain alive or if double frees occur, often revealing misuse of memory that leads to later panics.

By leveraging Zig's clear panic messages, pairing them with LLDB for live inspection, and augmenting your code with targeted `assert` statements or debug allocators, you transform runtime errors into actionable insights— ensuring that safety violations become teachable moments rather than baffling crashes.

D.3 Community Q&A and Best References

In the course of mastering Zig, you'll inevitably encounter questions that go beyond any one guide—whether it's the subtleties of cross-compiling to an exotic target, the right pattern for a custom allocator in a real-time system, or simply the most ergonomic way to structure your `build.zig`. Fortunately, Zig's community has coalesced around a handful of official venues where experts and newcomers alike gather to ask, answer, and archive the collective wisdom of the language.

Below is an official example drawn from the Zig website's Community page. It shows how the "Where to Ask" section describes the primary channels for real-time discussion and long-term reference:

```
Where to Ask:
  · Discord: https://zig.dev/discord (general chat, support channels, off-
topic)
```

· Zulip: https://ziglang.zulipchat.com (structured streams, RFC discussion)
· GitHub Discussions: https://github.com/ziglang/zig/discussions (release-specific Q&A)
· Stack Overflow: https://stackoverflow.com/questions/tagged/zig (indexed questions and answers)
· RFCs Repository: https://github.com/ziglang/rfcs (proposals, design rationale, deep dives)

In practice, you might hop onto Discord's `#help` channel to troubleshoot a build error and then migrate to Zulip's "Runners" stream to propose optimizations for `std.benchmark`. If you discover a nuanced bug in the standard library, you open a GitHub Discussion in the core repository or file an issue, citing your minimal reproducible case. When you want a polished, peer-reviewed solution, you search Stack Overflow for the `ziglang` tag and often find answers that have been refined over months or years.

As a concrete example, when a user recently ran into an unexpected "file not found" error on Windows, they posted their `build.zig` snippet and directory layout on GitHub Discussions, where a maintainer pointed out the need to call `exe.addIncludePath` with the Windows path-style backslashes. That thread now serves as the canonical reference for dozens of programmers facing cross-compile quirks on that platform.

By weaving together real-time chat for rapid feedback, structured threads for proposal debates, and indexed Q&A for long-term reference, the Zig community ensures that no question remains an island. As you continue your journey, bookmark these resources, participate in discussions, and consider contributing back your own solutions—so that the ecosystem grows ever more robust and welcoming.

www.ingramcontent.com/pod-product-compliance
Lightning Source LLC
Chambersburg PA
CBHW080554060326
40689CB00021B/4849